Dutch-born Brother Andre
President of Open Doors w
wide mission organisation
threatened Christians in E:
Latin America and the Middle East.

His first book, *God's Smuggler*, sold more than nine
million copies and has been translated into more than
eighteen languages.

Exiled Romanian pastor, Joseph Ton, described Brother
Andrew as 'the greatest Christian revolutionary of my
generation.'

He continued: 'Brother Andrew started taking Bibles into
Eastern Europe and then he began telling the stories in that
revolutionary book, *God's Smuggler*. It kindled the
imagination of everybody in the West. The idea became
exciting, thrilling, adventurous and just great as a service for
the Lord and the brethren in the East.

'And people found out that Christians in the East were not
dead. They were there, they were struggling, and most of all
they needed the Bible.

'The greatest thing that has happened to Eastern Europe
and the Communist countries in my generation is Brother
Andrew!'

Dan Wooding is a British journalist and writer who has
travelled extensively with Brother Andrew and other Open
Doors staff, seeing the work of the mission at first hand and
interviewing believers in countries like El Salvador and
Uganda, Poland and Cuba. He was a senior reporter with
both the *Sunday People* and the *Sunday Mirror*, two of
Europe's largest circulation newspapers. He is married to
Norma, and they have two sons, Andrew and Peter.

God's Agent

Brother Andrew with Dan Wooding

Marshall Pickering

Marshall Morgan & Scott
Pickering & Inglis
34-42 Cleveland Street, London W1P 5FB

Copyright © Brother Andrew with Open Doors International 1983
First published in 1983 by Marshall Morgan & Scott
Publications Ltd
Part of the Marshall Pickering Holdings Group

Reprinted 1987
Reissued in 1989

ISBN 0 551 01023 1

Some names and locations in this book have been changed for the
protection of those featured in these pages.

Printed and bound in Great Britain by
Courier International Ltd, Tiptree, Essex

Contents

1: War is declared

MY heart began to slam against the walls of my chest as I tiptoed along the darkened street and then edged my way down the driveway to a window of the hated S.S. man's house. I was on a mission for my country and I knew there was great danger involved.

Slowly, hardly daring to breathe, I peeped through the window of his detached house to a hallway where his family's clothing was hung up. My eyes darted from one item to another until I spotted it – the pistol that he so proudly wore as he strutted in his jackboots and green uniform through our little Dutch village of Witte. The gun was still invitingly housed in the belt that he wore as he strode around the village.

When I had first seen this hawk-faced Dutchman, one of thousands of my people who were shamefully collaborating with the Germans at that time during World War Two, I vowed that I would take this weapon from him and hand it over to my heroes in the local Dutch resistance.

A cold sweat broke out on my forehead as I silently opened the front door and heard laughter coming from the lounge. The collaborator and his family were obviously drinking coffee and had even been considerate enough to put the radio on to cover up the sound of my break-in.

I let myself in and, with an unbearable tension enveloping me, tiptoed towards the gun-belt. It was located just behind a door which, without warning, could open and bring me face-to-face with a member of the despised family. I knew only too well that if I was caught by any of them that confrontation could result in a sudden, painful death for me at the receiving end of the very weapon I was trying to relieve the S.S. man of.

With the deftness of one of Fagin's little thieves in Victorian London, I silently reached out and carefully extracted the weapon from its holster.

Fortunately, the laughter and conversation continued, but it was like a blur in my mind. As soon as I had my prize, I carefully closed the front door, took a deep breath and then took off like the wind down the cobbled street, zig-zagging from side to side to dodge the bullets that I imagined might come from anyone sympathetic to the Germans who had seen me emerging with the stolen gun.

Adrenalin spilled into my body as I rushed around corners faster than I had ever done before, the gun clasped tightly in my sweaty right palm. Soon I came to the garden of a friend and dived head first among the rhubarb. Breathing heavily, I lay there for several minutes firmly clasping the pistol that was destined for the Dutch resistance.

I had become one of their young recruits in the village and had pledged to play my part in the winning of World War Two by stealing as many German weapons and bicycles as possible. Then I would hand them over to these dare-devil fighters.

My resolve to continue my one-boy mission against the German invaders had hardened one Sunday night when, as I lay in bed, I heard the chilling crack of rifle shots.

Next morning my friend Peter had told me that a group of Dutch prisoners had been taken out by the railway station and executed in cold blood.

'But why?' I was puzzled.

'It's because members of the resistance had blown up a bridge. The Germans wanted to teach us all a lesson.'

I was so angry.

'Well, the only lesson I've learned is that I'm going to do even more to help the resistance,' I told Peter.

Under the cover of darkness, I took messages from one resistance group to another and eventually was trusted enough to be allowed to distribute, to a carefully selected band of villagers, the underground news sheet that was being produced.

Shortly after the robbery that night, I made my way to the Christian primary school where I knew a resistance cell was assembled. I tapped out the required code of knocks on the loft door and waited for a few moments.

Then Kees, an unshaven youth, opened up. His face quickly creased into a smile as he looked down at me and spotted what I held in my hand.

'Well done, young Andrew,' he said, reaching down to take the pistol. 'You've done well for your country. As a reward, you can come up here and join us. We're listening on our radio to the news from London on Radio Orange. Then Queen Wilhemina is due to make a special broadcast from England.'

I sat on the floor in a state of euphoria that, at last, I was one of 'them'. I would do anything for these few brave patriots to make life as difficult as possible for the German soldiers in our village. No task would be too dangerous for me.

I became especially accomplished at sabotaging German military cars. I would creep out of our tiny brick house clasping a bag of our precious rationed sugar. I knew Mama had suspicions that I was up to no good, but she was also secretly proud of my relationship with the local branch of the Dutch resistance.

'I see the lieutenant's staff car is having lots of problems these days,' observed Mama one day. 'He doesn't seem to be able to start it.'

She looked at me and smiled softly.

'You know what, Andrew?'

'What, Mama?'

'Someone told me today that he suspects that there was sugar in his petrol tank.'

I grinned as if butter wouldn't melt in my mouth and said nothing.

At the age of twelve, I had already learned many skills as a derring-do adventurer. Not the least was to be able to escape from the boredom of Sunday morning services without Mama and Papa realising it.

My blacksmith father was almost stone deaf. In fact he never once heard the throaty roar of the engines of the thousands of British and American bombers that flew over Witte to drop their load of death and destruction on many German cities.

Because of Papa's disability, the family would walk to the front pew of our church where a special telephone had been rigged up so that Papa could hear the preacher a little better. Fortunately the pew was too small for all of us to sit together, and so I would walk a little slower than my brother Bas and sisters Maartje and Geltje, allowing them and Mama and Papa to go up the aisle before me. (My elder brother Ben was not with us as he had gone into hiding with the resistance during the last years of the war.)

'Oh, I see the pew's full again,' I would say in apparent consternation. 'It looks like I will have to sit at the back again.'

Just as the first hymn in this Reformed Church was about to begin, I would slip outside. In the summer I would go into the beautiful wind-swept fields and let wild crows sit on my shoulders and peck at my ears. In the snow-covered winters, I would jog home to get my skates and cruise my way down nearby frozen canals.

Timing was the essence of my dodge-the-morning-service plan. I had an instinctive feeling when it was about to end and I would slip back into the vestibule just as the first of the solemn-faced 'sufferers' emerged from what I considered their torment. I'd ease myself close to them and listen out for comments about the sermon. Usually my young friends would also tell me something of what the preacher had spoken about. These snippets proved very useful because, without them, I could not have fulfilled the highlight of my week of adventure.

In my country it is the custom to meet in different private homes after morning service to drink coffee. The women would make it and the men drink it. As they did, they would also smoke cigars, and conduct a point-by-point assessment of the sermon. As the thick pungent smoke filled the room, I would join a group of men in their dark suits and make 'informed' comments about the sermon.

'I see that the preacher has used that text from 1 Corinthians, chapter thirteen, several times over the past few months', I would say, a hint of criticism in my voice.

'Yes,' would smile my Uncle Johan, 'you're right, Andrew. I'm glad you've taken such an interest in what he's been saying.'

He would pat me on the head.

'You're a good boy.'

With an angelic look, I would then move on to the next group. My parents never once suspected my little ploy.

But I could not always escape from hearing about the love of Jesus in my home; it was booming in each day on our crackly radio. Mama's health wasn't good, she had high blood pressure which made her very weak. So she would spend hours sitting in a chair, listening to the gospel station from Hilversum.

'Isn't that singing beautiful, Andrew?' she would smile at me.

I would nod my head, and mutter to myself, 'It may be beautiful to you, Mama, but it's plain torture to me. It's all so dull.'

* * *

I suppose I have always been a soldier at heart. I felt I needed a cause to fight for, a battle to win. That's why I played tricks on the enemy. When the Germans invaded Holland, my formal education ended. I was just twelve when soldiers took over the school building as their barracks. In my teens I had tried to learn machine fitting, but I found that completely boring.

One day I returned home from a run in the countryside when I found Papa working amongst the cabbages in our garden. As he saw me he straightened up slowly and fixed his blue eyes on mine. I knew instinctively that he was going to pull me up with a jolt.

'Andrew,' he boomed, not realising how his voice carried.

'Yes, Papa.'

'Look, my son, you are now sixteen years old. The war is over. What do you plan to do with your life?'

I shrugged sadly, 'I don't know Papa. I wish I did.'

As half the village tuned into our conversation, he gave me an ultimatum.

'Andrew,' he bawled as if speaking through a megaphone, 'it's time for you to choose a trade. By autumn I want your decision.'

One decision I had already come to was to leave home. I

knew that I couldn't bear to stay any longer in that poky little community whose life seemed to revolve around talking about the 'good old days'. Inhabitants in the village were getting older and older and not being replaced. As soon as the young people reached an age when they could fend for themselves, many of them left for a new life in one of the big cities.

Whenever I needed to think straight I would go on long runs. On one occasion I took off barefoot across the polders (reclaimed land) enjoying the exhilaration of seeing the lush green scenery bob by. The further I ran, the clearer my mind became. The exercise blew away the cobwebs.

After five miles, *it* suddenly came to me. I WOULD BECOME A SOLDIER! I'd serve my country by putting down an armed rebellion in the colonies. I had read in the papers that some of the people in the Dutch East Indies, which had recently been liberated from Japan, now wanted their independence after 350 years of Dutch rule.

'That's it. I'll teach those people a lesson they won't forget,' I shouted out to myself as I clambered up the dike that led me back to Witte.

Mother turned down the radio when I told her that I had an announcement to make.

'Mama, I'm going to be a soldier . . .'

Her face drained as pale as buttermilk.

'Oh, Andrew!' she gasped. 'Must we always think of killing?'

Fortunately, Papa and my brothers reacted differently to my decision and so, the following week, I borrowed my father's sturdy upright bicycle and headed towards the recruiting office in Alkmaar. As darkness fell, I was home again, but in a state of stark despair.

'They won't take me on until I'm seventeen,' I snapped at Ben when he queried my glum expression.

'Well, that's not too far away, Andrew. Just have a little more patience.'

Eventually, a few months later, I was proudly striding through the village in my new uniform. I was a servant of Queen Wilhelmina and would play my part in retaining our rebellious colony for the Crown.

Almost everyone in Witte warmly shook my hand and congratulated me on joining up; but, not Mr Whestra, a Christian man who had always taken a great interest in me.

'So, Andrew, you're off to the East Indies.'

I nodded proudly.

He fixed his gaze on mine.

'So you're off for adventure. I'll pray for you, Andrew. I'll pray that the adventure you find will satisfy.'

2: 'Get smart and lose your mind'

I COULD hardly contain my excitement as our transport ship, the *Sibajak*, landed in the Dutch East Indies, now known as Indonesia, just before Christmas, 1946. I was bowled over by the exotic sights that I beheld; the tropical smells; the near-naked porters carrying heavy loads up and down the gangplanks, their brown bodies glistening with perspiration; the hawkers screeching from the dockside for our attention.

I joined the crush of other young soldiers as I heaved my dufflebag onto my shoulders and struggled down the gangplank, desperately trying to shield my eyes from the fierce sun.

Around me clambered unarmed children and olive-skinned adults. Little did I realise that these were the sort of people I would soon be killing! A strange unease began to wrap itself around me. Then the heat, the stench, and the human anguish of their obvious poverty made me feel uneasy. I mopped my face awkwardly with my sleeve.

As I tried to gather my thoughts, I thought of Mama back home and how her eyes had brimmed with sadness and concern the day I had departed for the war in the east.

'Son,' she had said, as she reached under her apron and pulled out a small book, her personal Bible, 'I want you to have it. Please take it with you.'

What could I say to my mother? I promised that I would, knowing deep down that I was telling a lie. As I looked at her

I felt a sharp lance of guilt. Then I embraced her and put the Bible at the bottom of my dufflebag.

It didn't take long for us to be caught up in the adventure of war. We were rushing through jungles chasing slant-eyed guerrillas, our automatic rifles prepared for action. The war had become a colossal meat grinder, chewing up bodies from both sides at an enormous rate.

One day, during a break in killing, I turned to Hans, a young soldier from Rotterdam, and said: 'My friend, I've a new slogan for the Army.'

He lit up a cigarette and took a deep drag on it.

'What is it, Andrew?' he said as a trail of smoke snaked upwards from the ash.

I laughed.

'Join the Army and visit exotic places . . .' I paused and then, in a voice that suddenly became chilling, added: '*and kill exotic people!*'

He didn't smile.

'It's kill or be killed, isn't it, Andrew?' He was deadly serious. 'Anyway, we are doing it for our country – aren't we?'

I found that I soon began to enjoy the action – and the killing. No longer was I just aiming at paper targets, but at real, breathing human beings. Most of them didn't wear uniforms, but we were told that they were the *enemy*, so it didn't matter what we did as long as we got rid of them.

The excitement changed one day when an incident took place that has given me nightmares ever since. We were driving in convoy in trucks and jeeps through a small dusty village full of grass-roofed huts that were still partially inhabited. We became bold, thinking that the Nationalist guerrillas would not mine a village in which people were still living. These anti-personnel mines were something we all feared, because we knew that if we struck one we would be crippled for life, crippled, that is, if we were lucky and survived the explosion.

As we bumped along in our military vehicles, I looked at my young colleagues, their fingers poised on the triggers of their rifles, and I felt my nerves crank up another notch. Something inside me began to jangle an alarm. I was right, for suddenly there was a terrible explosion to my right and I saw my friend Arnie blown to smithereens. He had been riding a motorcycle that had hit a mine.

It was as if we all went berserk at the same moment. Like crazed, cornered animals we rained bullets all over the village. Our eyes were rolling wildly in their sockets, like those of fear-maddened horses, as we emptied our barrels at everything that moved. It was a wild display of destruction. When we finally stopped, several people lay silent and dead in front of us – all cut to ribbons by our torrent of bullets.

As I stumbled with my colleagues to the edge of the village I saw a sight that still haunts me. There was a young Indonesian mother lying on the ground in a pool of her own blood, her baby boy at her breast. Mother and child had been killed by the same bullet. A cloud of flies buzzed around their bullet-ridden corpses.

I felt like putting a bullet through my own brain there and then. What sort of person was I becoming that I could be involved in this kind of vile behaviour? I had turned into a vicious animal, hunting and being hunted. For a time I became a pacifist, resolving that, whatever the consequences to myself, I would not fire another shot in this brutal war.

But then, when another of my friends had been shot and killed by the guerrillas, I lined up for the next patrol to go after the enemy.

I suppose I eventually got a death wish. I found that I had

nothing to live for, especially after I had peeled open a letter from Ben, my elder brother.

I gasped with shock as I read: 'Mother's funeral was very moving . . .' What was he talking about? Funeral? What I had not realised was that Mother had died and Ben had written to me previously giving me the sad news. However, his letter had got lost.

'Oh no, not Mama.' I ran from my tent and straight into the forest, where I wept like a little child.

'God, why can't I die? Why can't one of those terrorists cut me down?' I was totally confused.

For the next few months, I got more crazy and dare-devilish. In combat I would wear a bright yellow straw hat which I looked upon as a dare and an invitation to the enemy that I was around.

'Shoot me if you can,' I would shout as I ran through the steaming jungles, my screams competing with the squawks of parrots and grunts of monkeys overhead. One day a bullet whistled through the crown of my hat, but I didn't care.

I enjoyed being the leader of the pack. When we went out on scouting missions, I would always lead the others. One day I was at least fifty yards ahead of the platoon, having almost jogged through a valley, when I literally ran over a ridge and smack into a group of ten guerrillas, all armed to the teeth.

What should I do? This was a no-win situation, I thought. So bluffing was the only answer.

'Drop your weapons,' I shouted at them. 'Your war is over. You are surrounded.'

Amazingly, they all dropped their weapons there and then and raised their hands in the air. I just stood there, my heart pounding, wondering whether they would realise that I had conned them into surrendering.

After what seemed like an eternity, my colleagues came over the ridge and gasped when they saw the sight ahead of them.

'Andrew, you're something else,' said the captain as the other soldiers took the group captive.

Our camp bulletin board carried a slogan that we had invented, which read, 'Get smart – lose your mind.'

My life had become a series of insane extremes. We fought like lunatics, and drank until we could hardly stand up. We would literally 'lose our minds' as we staggered from bar to bar, hurling our empty beer bottles through the windows of local stores.

After two years I began to feel my defiance deserting me. But still I went through the usual ritual of wearing my yellow straw hat and shouting and cursing as I roared after the terrorists.

My war eventually ended on the morning of February 12, 1949, on the outskirts of the capital, Djakarta. I was blasting away at the enemy when I suddenly realised that we were in deep trouble.

'Hey, Andrew, they're on three sides,' one of my colleagues hissed to me with fear in his voice. 'It'll take a miracle if we get out of this alive.'

Perspiration ran down my face into my eyes as I looked death in the face and was terrified because I didn't know what lay beyond it. Suddenly there was a blinding sizzle of yellow fire and a bullet flashed out of the bushes and smashed through my right ankle and out again. A bright dart of pain shot up my leg. I couldn't believe it at first. I stood frozen for a long moment, then I sank into the water of the paddy field in which we were fighting. There I sat, blinking, not totally comprehending what had happened. I looked down at my right combat boot and saw a gaping hole with blood oozing down into the water, making it run red.

'I'm hit,' I murmured in a voice of strained agony. 'Please help me . . . someone.'

A couple of medics silently slipped beside me and quickly eased my body on to a stretcher and then crawled along in the water bearing me in a way that meant all that was visible to the enemy at the top of the rice field dike was *me*. Bullets whistled at my prostrate form, but fortunately did not make contact with me.

I came to, still wearing my yellow straw hat, stretched out in the operating table in a Djakarta evacuation hospital.

'I think we should try and save the leg first, but we may have to amputate,' I heard the doctor telling the nurse. 'The joint is just one big mess.'

For two hours my ankle was operated on with just a local anaesthetic to try vainly to keep the searing pain from my brain. As my ankle was sewn up with a needle and twine, I was suddenly aware that I was bare-headed.

'Nurse,' I whispered anxiously, 'my hat. Where's my hat?'

She stooped down and picked it up from underneath the operating table and gently put it back on my head.

'Thank you, nurse,' I smiled. 'I don't feel fully dressed if I am not wearing it.'

I paused for a moment as the waves of pain just kept coming.

Then I added, 'You know, we were supposed to have been the boys who got smart and lost our minds.'

By now my voice was high, cracking. 'I didn't even get my brains blown out. Just my foot!'

What a farce this was all turning out to be. I had tried 'real adventure' and discovered that it was nothing but a hoax. There was *no* real adventure, it was all a grand illusion.

And the price of my searching? At the tender age of twenty, I was destined to be a cripple for life.

3: The monkey and the coconut

IN a brief second, I had been turned into a hopeless wreck. That made me both angry and frightened. I lay on my bed at night having sweaty, ugly nightmares which often involved *that* mother and baby in the East Indies.

During the day, I would take deep breaths and clench and unclench my right fist. I was fighting anger and confusion. Life seemed so pointless.

I spent much of my time writing long letters to pen pals all over Holland. During my time in the East Indies, I had managed to acquire some seventy-two pen pals – many through the Dutch Red Cross. There had been a method in the madness, however, because this meant that I was not only assured of a steady stream of letters from the Mother-land, but also food parcels as well.

My favourite correspondent was Thile, a petite, raven-haired girl whom I had met at a Reformed Church back home. Thile had promised to keep in touch with me and I had been writing to her during my whole time in Indonesia.

Black despair pressed behind my eyes one day, shortly before I was shot when, bewildered and bitter, I put into words my deepest loathings about myself. I told Thile how bad I really was and how my thoughts and actions were often very wicked. It was the sort of letter you only pen to get rid of your pent-up frustrations.

At the end of the depressing letter I admitted: 'I have no desire for God. I don't want to pray. Instead of going to church I go to the pub and drink until I don't give a hoot.'

I wrote this letter not meaning to send it. It really was just for my benefit. When I was rushed into hospital, my comrades went through my belongings and found the letter. Assuming I had forgotten to post it, they did just that.

Thile was shocked when she received it. Nevertheless, she wrote back to me. It was a wonderful letter in which she said that however bad and sinful I felt, Jesus understood and would still accept me.

'He wants you just as you are, Andrew,' she wrote.

During one particularly anguished time I was thrashing around on my bed when my hand fell on a book.

'What's this?' I said as I picked it up and tried to focus my eyes on it.

'Mama's Bible . . . what's it doing here?'

A nurse came over and clasped my hand.

'Andrew, your friends found it in the bottom of your duffelbag. They didn't know if you wanted it, but they left it in anyway.'

'Thanks . . .' I stammered. 'Maybe I'll read it one day.'

The hospital was run by Franciscan sisters, and it wasn't long before I fell head over heels in love with all of them as they cheerfully went about their duties in their uncomfortable starched white habits. They were so lovely as they laughed and sang their way around the wards. And that despite the fact that they worked from dawn until night. Florence Nightingale would have been proud of them as they cheerily cleaned out bedpans, dressed wounds, and wrote letters for us. They even bought us cigarettes.

One day, my favourite nun, Sister Patrice, bathed me.

'Sister,' I asked, 'how can you and the other nuns be so cheerful in the midst of such suffering?'

Her eyes were bright with enthusiasm.

'Andrew,' she replied, 'you ought to know the answer to that – a good Dutch boy like you. It's the love of Christ.'

Then she spied the Bible that still lay unopened at my

bedside.

'You have no need to ask, do you?' she continued, tapping the Holy Book. 'You've got the answer right there.'

When she had left, I picked up Mama's Bible which had remained a closed book to me for two and a half years and began slowly reading through it. I began at Genesis 1.1 and read the story of creation and how sin came into the world. Then Exodus, Leviticus . . . Matthew . . . Revelation.

Day after day, as I lay still, my leg encased in plaster, I found I couldn't put this book down. It was a thriller, a romance, a love story, all wrapped into one.

'You know, sister, the Bible really *is* a love story . . . the story of God's love for mankind,' I told my Franciscan friend one day.

She smiled knowingly.

I knew that Thile, back home, was a Christian, so I began anxiously filling pages with questions on the Scriptures for her to answer. I knew she would reply to those she could, and go to her pastor for answers to others.

So began an extraordinary across-the-oceans Bible correspondence course between the East Indies and Holland.

But still I harboured a bitterness about what I had suffered. I could see the joy of the Franciscan nuns and in Thile's letters, but I couldn't let go of something, though, at that time, I didn't know exactly what it was.

'Andy, now the plaster's off, we'll be shipping you back home,' announced Sister Patrice, one day.

'But I want to tell you a story that I think you should hear and act upon.'

I listened patiently as she told of how the natives of Indonesia cash in on the fact that a monkey will never let go of something it wants, even if it means losing his freedom or very life.

'Andrew,' she said gently, 'they take a coconut and make a

hole in one end just big enough for a monkey's paw to slip through. Then they drop a pebble into the opening and wait in the bushes with a net.

'Sooner or later one of these curious old monkeys will come along. He will pick up that shell and begin to shake it. He'll look inside. Then he'll slip his paw into the hole and begin to feel around until he gets that pebble. But when he tries to bring it out he discovers that he can't get his paw through the hole without letting go'

By now her face was deadly serious.

'Andrew, that monkey will not let go of what he thinks is a prize. It's the easiest thing in the world to capture someone who acts like that.'

I knew what she was then going to say.

'Andrew, are you desperately clinging on to something? Something that is keeping you from your freedom?' Her blue eyes held my gaze as if to emphasise what she had just said and it was a revelation to me. I was hanging on to an illusion of happiness that hadn't worked for me, but still I couldn't bear to become a Christian. It was pride. After all, those believers I knew in Holland were such dull people.

The next day was my twenty-first birthday, and I was *going home*. As a special farewell celebration I brought together all the survivors who were still able to limp or walk from the company with which I had come to the war-torn land three years previously.

There were eight of us and we got rip-roaring drunk. We sat in that run-down bar full of thick tobacco smoke and the smell of spilled booze, and shouted, cursed, and tried to numb the terrible feelings we had about life and death!

'Here's to those who've already gone in the fighting,' I shouted near the end of the proceedings.

'Let's hope they haven't gone to hell!'

At last I'd got smart and lost my mind!

4: Real adventure

MY hands began to shape a vase out of sticky, but pliable clay. It was difficult work.

'The trick, Andrew,' explained the instructor, Mr Cor Viser, at the veterans' hospital at Doorn, is to put the lump of clay at the centre of the potter's wheel. Then keep the wheel turning with your foot control while your fingers work it into whatever shape you want.'

It was easy for him to explain, but he didn't know the agony I suffered as my damaged right foot tried to turn the control and my hands attempted to form some kind of recognisable shape from the clay.

'Andrew, I know you are only doing this to strengthen your ankle, but please try and get your clay to turn into something that we can all recognise, not just the formless mess it is right now.'

One day, as he turned to walk away after delivering another tirade, I got so angry that I picked up my half-formed wet clay and hurled it at Jaap, another injured soldier who was sitting next to me.

It clumped solidly into the side of his head and began dripping down his face.

I held my hands up in horror when I realised what I had done.

'I'm so sorry, my friend,' I said. 'I forgot myself.'

Jaap smiled wistfully.

'It's all right, Andrew. I understand your frustrations. It's not easy for any of us . . .'

During one home leave I went to see Thile. She looked as beautiful as ever with those large, appealing hazel eyes and black, shoulder-length hair.

'Thile, I don't know how to tell you this, but my relationship with God is non-existent,' I told her sadly, as I painfully limped beside her. 'I don't know if I even believe.'

She took my hand and stared out across the harbour full of bobbing fishing boats, then laughed nervously.

'God hasn't come to a standstill you know, Andrew. I think you're like one of your own lumps of clay. He has a plan for you and he's trying to get you into the centre of it, but you keep dodging and slithering away.'

Then she turned her wide eyes on mine. 'Andrew, you cannot guess what he has in mind for you. It could be the Lord wants to shape you into something wonderful.'

I managed to change the subject and Thile kindly didn't say any more.

I couldn't imagine how God, if he actually did exist, could possibly do anything with someone as physically and mentally broken as I was.

As I limped back towards the stop where I would get the bus to the hospital, I thought of the first time I had visited mother's grave. Papa had got me to sit on his bicycle seat and had pushed me the half mile to the cemetery. He knew I couldn't have made it by myself.

Tears welled up in my eyes as I read her name on the white gravestone. Then I saw the Scripture verse underneath her name which said, 'Blessed are the dead which die in the Lord, says the Spirit, for their works will follow them.'

I turned to Papa and said, 'That is so apt for Mama. She had so many good works.'

A lump came in Papa's throat as he tried to smile at me.

A short time later, I was enveloped in another terrible

depression. I was wrestling in my mind about whether I had any faith in God, if he actually existed and whether my life had any future at all. I somehow dragged myself back to the cemetery and, in the dead of night, flung myself prostrate on the cold grave.

'Mother, mother, can't you hear me? Please say something . . . please,' I cried out.

She didn't reply; she was elsewhere.

★　★　★

It was on a cold, gusty mid-morning in September 1949, that a pretty blonde came into our ward and invited all twenty of us to a tent meeting in the town. A bus, she told us, would arrive at seven p.m. to transport us there.

She was extremely shy and made her escape from us to a hail of wolf-whistles, her cheeks as red as a beetroot.

Pier, my friend in the next bed, thought it would be good for us to celebrate our outing that night and so he slipped down to the village and came back with two small bottles of gin. We took turns in gulping it down.

'This will get us in the right spirits for tonight, eh, Andrew?' chuckled a befuddled Pier as he took another swig of gin from his bottle.

'Shoooooould do . . .' I slurred back, by now happily inebriated.

Pier and I sat at the back of the vast tent, our bottles tucked away in our inside pockets. After a few swigs, enjoyed behind the protection of our sleeves, we began heckling all who spoke.

A thin-faced man with deep-set eyes became so disturbed with our behaviour, that he got up on the platform and held up his hand.

'My friends,' he said, solemnly, 'there are two people here tonight who are bound by powers they cannot control.'

Then, closing his eyes, he began to pray for us. As he did, we held our stomachs to suppress our laughter until our insides began to ache from our efforts. Suddenly the congregation started to sing again, and we again collapsed. Tears rolled down our faces. I hadn't laughed so much for years. Looking back now, however, I know it was a manic form of laughter.

Still the weasel-faced man droned on. He finally admitted defeat by giving up his urgent supplications for us.

'As our brethren over whom foreign spirits have gained influence will not be quiet, we had better sing another song,' he announced.

Our chortles were soon drowned out by the singing of 'Let My People Go'. Then something strange took place. The words that boomed out under the tent began to burn into my mind. I became serious and, as I did, the words 'Let them go . . . let me go . . .' continued to bore into me.

As the bus took us back to the centre, those words '. . . let *me* go . . .' kept spinning around my head.

Next day, back at the potter's wheel, another surprise took place. Although I had a terrible hangover and my mouth was as dry as sawdust, I somehow did a marvellous job with the grey clay on the wheel. Time and time again I worked my foot slowly and vase after vase rose up under my fingers.

It was even more unsettling when I lay on my bed during the rest period and picked up Mama's Bible. I had not read it since I had returned to my homeland but now I began flicking through the pages. I stopped from time to time to read parts of the Scriptures that caught my eye. I found I couldn't put it down. Passages that I had never understood before suddenly became crystal clear.

A week later, a nurse came over to me and announced, 'Andrew, I have good news for you. You are making such good progress that we have decided you can begin to go home for long weekends.'

Back home, I would lie for hours on my bed in the attic 'devouring' Mama's Bible.

'What on earth is happening to you?' enquired my sister Geltje one day, as she entered the room with a steaming bowl of soup.

'I don't know, sister, but whatever it is, it's something I can't stop . . .'

I was soon limping to church, not only for the Sunday morning service but in the evening as well.

When I was eventually formally mustered out of the army in November 1949, I decided to buy myself a bicycle with part of my demobilisation pay. I felt the exercise would help with my rehabilitation and strengthen my withered right leg. I was still having problems walking properly, but with two wheels below me, I would become more mobile and get lots of exercise at the same time.

I would cycle to other towns to attend church services there. One Tuesday I pedalled all the way to Amsterdam to a Baptist service. Every night of the week I would find a service and arrive, armed with a Bible, plus a notebook and pencil. I would take down all that the preacher said, and then would look up the passages in the Bible next morning to check that all he had quoted were really there.

One day my other sister, Maartje, came up the ladder leading to the attic bedroom with a cup of tea for me. She looked concerned.

'Andrew, all the family are getting very worried about you. Papa thinks you are suffering from shell shock . . .'

Maartje saw my anguished look and laughed in a nervous, keyed-up way. Then she quickly backed down the steps.

As she did, I began musing aloud.

'Am I really becoming a religious fanatic? Am I losing my

mind?' I had heard of people who had really flipped and went around quoting the Bible at everyone. My mind began working restlessly, looking for some way out.

Several months later something happened to me that was even more radical than that bullet that ripped through my ankle in the East Indies. I was in bed on a freezing January night in 1950 as sheets of icy sleet blew across the polders and flew against my windows. I pulled the blankets under my chin to try and keep warm. I shut my eyes and could hear voices swirling around in the wind. There was Sister Patrice saying, 'The monkey will never let go . . .' Then I heard the singing in the marquee, 'Let *my* people go . . . let *me* go . . .'

I suddenly shouted out loud, 'What am I hanging on to? Or is something holding on to me? God I want freedom.'

As the rest of my family lay soundly asleep, I turned and leaned back on the bed and stared at the darkened ceiling. Quietly, suddenly, I let go of my inner man, my ego. Everything became startlingly clear. This was the missing piece in the puzzle I had been trying to solve. I *had* to turn myself over to God.

'Lord,' I said simply, 'if you will show me the way, I will follow you.' At that moment I knew that I had handed myself totally over to the Lord.

At last I was on the road to real adventure!

5: Jumping over dustbins

THE implications of my simple prayer really hit me next morning as I went out into the cobbled streets of the village. For, despite the sharp morning chill, a hot triumphant joy coursed through my veins and I couldn't contain my excitement. I spotted dustbins left out for emptying and, one by one, I jumped over all of them. For the first time in my life I felt intensely alive. It was a happiness that not even my still painful ankle could interfere with.

A grin as big as a Cheshire cat's played about my lips. It was so wide that it prompted a neighbour to come over to me and ask, 'Andrew, what has happened to you?'.

'I can't explain it . . .'

'Well, it must have been something big, you look so different.' With that he warmly pumped my hand.

I immediately had a great thirst to know more about God and his plan for my life. So when I heard that there was to be a tent meeting nearby I went along with Kees, my friend. The rally was led by Arne Donker, a well-known Dutch evangelist. Before he preached, Donker invited a middle-aged lady sitting beside him to 'give a word about your work for the Lord in the slums of Paris.'

This small but dynamic lady, who turned out to be a relative of Corrie ten Boom, author of the best-selling book, *The Hiding Place*, asked us to open our Bibles to Galatians, chapter 6, verse 7. Then she began reading 'Be not deceived; God is not mocked: for whatsoever a man soweth, that shall he also reap.'

She put down her Bible on the podium and began telling the story of a man who worked in Paris at the end of the last century.

'His job was to lay down cobbles in the streets of the French capital,' she said in a penetrating voice that commanded instant attention. 'It was hard work and, one night, he became so tired that, just before darkness descended, he decided to go home. He still had a few more cobbles to lay, but that job could wait until the next morning.

'That night a horse and carriage came along the very street where he had been working and the horse tripped in the hole that he hadn't filled up. The driver was thrown to the ground and instantly killed.

'The dead man left behind a wife and two daughters. Because there was no social security in those days and, therefore, no income coming in, the two girls were forced out on to the streets to become prostitutes. It was the only way they could earn money.

'The mother died of TB and malnutrition a few months later.

'The girls, because of their indecent work, soon led many men astray and were responsible for the break-up of several marriages,' she continued as every eye in the tent was riveted on her. 'The circle of their bad influence just got wider and wider.'

The Dutch missionary paused, as if to add emphasis to what she was about to say. Then she seemed to look straight at me.

'Who do you think was responsible for that terrible situation that affected hundreds of people? Of course it was the man who didn't finish his job properly.'

The missionary peered over the top of her spectacles.

'I read to you earlier that "whatsoever a man soweth, that shall he also reap." On the Day of Judgment, an army of people could stand before you and accuse you of not finishing the job that God has given you to do. For instance, a man might stand before you and say, "I accuse you." You might retort, "But I never knew you." That will not make any difference. That fact was that you did not finish the job entrusted to you and the ripple effect of that will spread to hundreds, thousands or even millions of people.'

With that she sat down. I was absolutely stunned. For a time I didn't hear what Arnie Donker was saying. All I could think of was being accused by someone on the Judgment Day for not completing the task God wanted me to do.

I was finally jolted back into the reality of the meeting, when Mr Donker leaned over the podium and said: 'Friends, I've had the feeling all night that something very special is going to happen at this meeting. Someone out there in the audience wants to give himself to the mission field.'

Kees and I looked at each other. We knew that God was speaking to us and so we rose to our feet at exactly the same time. Every eye in the tent had homed in on us. I couldn't believe that I was there on my knees at the front next to Kees as Mr Donker said a prayer over us.

But there was even worse to come.

'Now boys,' he said, clasping his large black Bible, 'I want you to go back to your own village and next Saturday turn up in front of your own church and we will all hold an open-air service.

'Kees, you will speak on "He sought me". Andrew, your text will be, "He found me", and then I'll conclude with, "He made me free".

'You'll be following the Biblical pattern – Jesus told the disciples to spread the good news "beginning at Jerusalem". They had to start their preaching in their own backyard.'

We looked at each other in dismay. Didn't he know what

he was asking? We would be laughed out of Witte. I felt a burning sensation at the back of my neck.

'The only people who hold open-air-services outside the church are usually looked upon as cranks from out of town,' I told Kees.

'Well,' he responded, 'that's not necessarily a bad thing. If we don't tell anyone in the village that we are going to speak, they'll just assume it's the usual open-air service and hardly anyone will turn up.'

I began writing out my little speech and memorising it. Then I stood in front of the mirror practising what I would say.

On the Saturday evening, I made my way to the church. I felt quite nervous but when I saw the huge crowd that was already assembled, my nervousness turned to stark terror. What were they all doing there? Among them were relatives and those whom I looked upon as foes.

'Oh, we heard you and Kees were going to speak,' explained one neighbour. 'We've never had anyone from the village do anything like this before.'

I felt my face turn blood-red with embarrassment. My knees were knocking like never before. When it came my turn to speak, I stood on a little portable pulpit that Arne Donker had brought with him. At first my words came out slow and considered. Then I threw away my notes and just told everyone how I had felt so guilty and dirty coming home from the war in the East Indies.

'I carried around a terrible burden about what I was and what I wanted out of life . . .' By now my knees had stopped knocking and there was complete silence as many looked on with rapt attention. Heads began to nod with understanding.

'It all changed one night recently during a storm when I laid down that burden of guilt at the feet of Jesus.'

My public testimony began to flow out faster and faster,

everything I had kept bottled up tumbled out, until words were falling helter-skelter.

Then I turned to Mr Donker and explained, with a smile on my face, that he had got me to say I wanted to become a missionary.

My face lit up with joy as I added, 'I might surprise him at that . . .'

★   ★   ★

I excitedly tore open the telegram and read it out loud to myself, 'Regret to inform you expected vacancy has not materialised. Request for admission denied. You may re-apply 1954.'

I could hardly believe my eyes.

'But, Lord there must be a mistake.' I went over in my mind how I had gone out one Sunday afternoon in September 1952 on to the polders where I could pray aloud without embarrassment. As I sat on the edge of a canal I had talked to God as I would have done my girlfriend – in a sincere but casual way. One-to-one.

'Lord I know there are problems. You know I can't really speak much English and if I went to that college in Glasgow, I would have to study that difficult language.

'And, of course, I can't even walk more than a hundred yards with this gammy leg of mine.

'But, if it is your will, I am willing to trust you.'

Then, with an air of finality, I added. 'Whenever, wherever, however you want me, Lord, I'll go. And I'll begin this very minute. Lord, as I stand up from this place, and as I take my first step forward, will you consider that this is a step towards complete obedience to you?' I called it the 'Step of Yes'.

With that I stood up and gingerly took a step forward.

Suddenly, incredibly, there was a sharp twist in my lame ankle. I thought for a moment I had done even more damage to it. I screwed up my face as I carefully put the foot to the ground. It held me fine. What had happened? Slowly I began walking home, and as the leaves crunched agreeably under my feet, a verse of Scripture fixed itself in my mind: 'Going they were healed.' Although my one leg was thinner than the other, I knew that because I had agreed to 'Go', God had healed me.

So to prove to the world what had happened, that night I walked four miles to a youth meeting. My weakened right leg did hurt a bit, but the joy in my heart overcame that.

'Andrew, you look exhausted, let me take you home on my motor bike,' said a friend after the meeting.

I shook my head.

'No thanks, Leo, I've got another four miles to walk for Jesus.'

Next morning two more important things happened. First, at the chocolate factory where I worked, I felt a strange sensation in my ankle. When I took off my shoe and sock I discovered that the stitches in my damaged ankle had come out – and the terrible wound had completely healed up.

Then, after work that day I applied to the college in Glasgow run by the Worldwide Evangelisation Crusade – a mission that trained missionaries to go out to parts of the world where the churches didn't have programmes.

Sidney Wilson, a Scottish evangelist I had got to know, had explained to me that the mission had been founded by Englishman C. T. Studd, a former international cricketer who had given up his career to serve God in China and later Africa. Mr. Wilson told me that if the W.E.C. thought God wanted a person in a certain place, they would send him there and trust God to worry about the details.

He continued: 'If they think a man has a genuine call and a

deep enough commitment, they don't care if he hasn't a degree to his name. They train him at their own school for two years and then send him out.'

W.E.C. appealed to me, so I applied.

But now came this bombshell. They couldn't fit me in. However, I knew this telegram wasn't the end of the matter. After all, *I* had heard that little voice I had come to recognise as God's. He had told me to 'Go', so I would do just that! I sold things like my bicycle and my much-valued shelf of books and bought a one-way rail and boat ticket to London, where I could meet with the heads of the W.E.C. before going north to Glasgow.

'But didn't you get our cable?' The man at the headquarters in south London looked at me in mute surprise as I stood at the front door.

'We sent you a telegram three days ago to say that there was no room up in Glasgow right now.'

'Yes, sir, but I came anyway.'

His face suddenly creased into a smile as I added, 'A place will open up for me when the time comes. I am certain of it. I just want to be here and ready.'

So I was allowed to stay and work there until a vacancy became available at the missionary training college.

★ ★ ★

It was at the headquarters that I first came into contact with William Hopkins, one of the most extraordinary men I had ever met. At our initial introduction the first thing I noticed about him was not that he was balding, and had a pronounced middle-age spread, but that his eyes sparkled mischievously.

As we were introduced by the W.E.C. director, he thrust forward his hand and shook mine warmly. Both his huge hands were wrapped around mine with such power that I winced, thinking he might even break my fingers.

'He looks strong enough,' said this unusual Englishman as he eyed me up and down. 'If I can get his work papers, he will do very well.'

I was puzzled, so the director explained that I would now have to leave the headquarters building – which, incidentally, had been constructed by Mr Hopkins, a building contractor – and I would be moving in with him and his wife.

As I quickly threw my toothbrush and razor and a few clothes into my battered suitcase, he smiled warmly at me.

'Andrew,' he said, rubbing his stubbled chin, 'I want you to call me Uncle Hoppy. My wife should be addressed as Mother Hoppy.'

I soon learned that Uncle Hoppy gave ninety per cent of his income to various missions. And whenever he found a tramp in need of accommodation, he just took him home with him and he and Mrs Hopkins cared for that down-and-out.

When I first arrived at their home in Northfleet, Kent, I was greeted by 'Mother Hoppy' who told me not to bother to go up to my room.

'The reason,' she explained a hint of weariness in her voice, 'is that there's a drunk in your bed.'

Uncle Hoppy's eyes twinkled as he looked at me.

'Don't worry, Andrew, you can sleep on the floor tonight. The life of a missionary can be a tough one.'

When it came time to bed down, he threw a couple of heavy overcoats over me.

'They'll keep you warm for a few hours,' he winked.

At four a.m. I heard the sound of water running in the bathroom. Some minutes later Uncle Hoppy came into my room. He looked blue with cold as he handed me a cup of tea.

As I wiped the sleep from my eyes, I asked, 'Are you all right, Uncle Hoppy? You look absolutely freezing!'

He grinned, though his teeth were still chattering.

'I'm all right, Andrew, I always have a cold bath first thing to thoroughly wake me up for my two-hour "quiet time" with the Lord.'

With that he went to a spare room and sank to his knees and began interceding for people and missions around the world.

Uncle Hoppy was definitely one of God's 'peculiar people'. He ran a storefront mission but it was rare that anyone ever passed through the doorway to attend the Sunday services. The doors were always left open and sometimes a stray derelict would wander in for a snooze and some warmth, but usually that was it.

One Sunday evening I went along with Uncle Hoppy to be greeted again by empty chairs.

'Right, Andrew,' he said, 'you sit in the front row and I'll begin.'

With that he announced the first hymn and we lustily sang together. Then he gave me an opening prayer, and another hymn. Soon came the announcements and then the offering. I dropped a few pence into the plate he shoved in front of me.

'Right, Andrew, now you come and preach.'

I was confused.

'But Uncle Hoppy, there's only you and me here . . .' I protested.

He looked sternly at me.

'Preach! You have to learn obedience to the one God has put over you.'

With that I took my place in the pulpit and preached to Uncle Hoppy and a room full of chairs. My text was rather foolishly, 'Thy faith hath saved thee.' With my still poor English pronunciation I kept stumbling over the words which came out something like, 'Dy fate has saved dee.'

There was certainly never a dull moment with Uncle Hoppy. When a tramp would stop him in the street and ask for money, he would immediately dig deep into his pocket and hand over some cash.

'But Uncle Hoppy, he will only use it to buy more booze,' I would protest.

My English friend looked at me, as if I shouldn't have questioned his action.

'Andrew, the Bible tells us to give to those that ask, and that's what I'm doing. You should always do the same. Don't question their motives.'

Although I never altogether understood the thinking and actions of Uncle Hoppy, I came to love him and his wife deeply. And when at last a letter came from Glasgow to say that a vacancy had opened up for me for the Autumn term, we did a celebrative march around Mother Hoppy's bed.

So finally in September 1953 I got on the train at London's Euston Station bound for Scotland – and my missionary training.

6: A knife at my throat

OVER the entrance of the W.E.C. college at Number 10 Prince Albert Road, Glasgow, on a wooden archway, were painted the words, 'Have Faith in God'.

The director, Stewart Dinnen, told me at the formal introduction, 'Andrew, the real purpose of this training is to teach our students that they can trust God to do what he has said he would do. We don't go from here into the traditional missionary fields, but into new territory. Our graduates are on their own. They cannot be effective if they are afraid, or if they doubt that God really means what he says in his word. So here we teach not so much ideas as trusting. I hope this is what you are looking for in a school, Andrew.'

I nodded enthusiastically. Here, at last, I was facing true adventure . . . with God at the helm.

*   *   *

Part of our training was to go out into the Glasgow slums and share the 'Good News' with the people of those areas. My little mission field was Partick, easily one of the most violent neighbourhoods of this Scottish city. It was so bad at that time that policemen would not go in there alone. People were being murdered in Partick almost every day.

But I really believed this was the area that God had called me to work in, and so I would go into those dark, dank, depressing housing estates where all the light bulbs had been broken or stolen. On every corner stood a shabby tavern where men would get hopelessly drunk on neat whisky and wives would cry because there was no money left for food or clothing. I would go into these dirty Dickensian hostelries to try and talk with some of the men and also give out tracts. I always asked permission from the pubs' proprietors. They never refused because I am sure they had consciences about what they were doing.

In one smoke-filled bar I met Jack Kearney, a hard-drinking Scotsman with whom I struck up an immediate conversation.

'Come and see me tomorrow at my place, laddie,' he slurred as he stumbled out clasping a tract that I had given him.

I invited Albert, a fellow-student from the Worldwide Evangelisation Crusade College, to come with me to see Jack. Full of trepidation, we picked our way along the threatening streets and up the pitch-black staircase to his fourth-floor apartment. As we climbed upwards we tripped over all sorts of garbage that had been left rotting on the stairs. Jack blinked through an alcoholic haze when he saw us at the door.

'Come in,' he motioned. When we got inside that darkened room which was lit by one naked bulb, we were horrified to see the state of the room. Wallpaper peeled from the wall, paint peeled from the ceiling and the sink was full of unwashed cups and plates.

I had hoped that by now he would have sobered up, but he was as drunk as ever. Suddenly he urinated in the sink.

'I'll fix up a cup of tea,' he then told us, picking up a couple of the unwashed cups from that sink. My stomach retched, but I knew I couldn't refuse.

'Lord, please help me not to be sick,' I prayed as I was eventually handed the nauseous brew.

As we talked, Jack turned his rough unshaven face towards me, and said, 'Hey Dutchman, you tell me you used to be in the army. What's the first law of war?'

I thought for a moment, and then replied, 'It's your life or mine. That's the law of war.'

'Right . . .' he said. 'Too right.'

I sat transfixed as he went over to a drawer, opened it and pulled out a large cut-throat razor. Slowly, deliberately, he unsheathed it and came for me.

By now, as he spoke, his eyes rolled ominously. 'I'm going to kill you,' he suddenly screamed as he stood in front of me and held the razor at my throat. A petrified Albert stayed in his seat and prayed as he had never done before.

I managed to gasp out, 'Yes Jack, it is my life or yours, and because of that you can't do this. Someone has already died to save both your life and mine.

'His name is Jesus Christ.'

I quickly continued. 'Look, Jack, Jesus came into the world because of these laws of war and because of the spiritual warfare where only one can win and the other must lose.

'One has to die so the other will live. That's exactly what Jesus Christ did.'

Jack still held the sharp edge so it just nicked the skin of my throat, so I kept talking about how Jesus had shed his blood that we both might live, and of the forgiveness that he offered.

'He died so you might live, Jack.'

Slowly, but surely, he withdrew the razor and stepped back, looking at me incredulously. He couldn't believe what I had told him. Then he folded it away and put it in the cupboard.

Feeling that maybe I shouldn't take the matter any further, I said breathlessly, 'Jack, that is just fine. Thank you for putting the razor away. We will leave now, but we'll come back to speak more about Jesus.'

Albert and I almost ran out of the place. We were ashen-faced and shaken, but grateful to the Lord that it hadn't been any worse.

I decided that I shouldn't take Albert with me on my next visit. I was afraid that if the same thing happened again, Albert might not be able to constrain himself and would try to intervene. This, I was sure, would certainly guarantee my bloody death. So I went alone.

Still dishevelled, but thankfully not drunk, Jack answered the door and invited me in.

'I'm so sorry about the other night. It was a terrible thing I did to you,' he said shamefacedly. 'It's the drink, you know. It makes me do terrible things.'

I told him that it was all right, that I really did understand.

'Jesus still loves you, Jack. Why don't you just pray and ask him into your life? He can change all of this.'

Jack suddenly sank to his knees and, in a childlike manner, poured out his heart to Jesus and asked him to forgive him and accept him just as he was. 'I'm a rotten person Jesus, but I want to follow you – if you'll have me,' he prayed.

Jesus did, and his life was transformed there and then. It was an incredible moment for both of us.

* * *

After all that I had done in earlier years, I was surprised that I still had a conscience. But I had, and it began to trouble me during a Wesleyan Holiness Convention at the Metropolitan Mission in Glasgow in July, 1953. I was really there to seek the power of the Holy Spirit in my life. I knew that it was imperative that I have more power to progress as a Christian.

'Lord,' I prayed, hands stretched upwards, 'please fill me with your Holy Spirit.'

Shortly afterwards, I was in a Glasgow park. It was early in the morning and no one else was around. As the sun was rising, I got down by the side of a bench and again began seeking the Holy Spirit to fill and purify me. Even as I prayed I knew that there was something vital that was keeping me from that infilling.

I felt a terrible conviction about unconfessed sins that, as a boy, I had committed. My face went hot with shame.

'Lord,' I said, 'I pledge here and now to put those sins right.'

As I rose to my feet I felt my heart suddenly become light and peaceful and I knew that God had filled me with his Holy Spirit. I wiped my eyes, which were misty with tears.

Right ahead I suddenly spotted a man hoisting the British Union flag. To me it was a confirmation that at last God had accepted my pledge and rewarded me in this wonderful way.

The first 'crime' I knew I had to put right was against my elder brother Ben. I always thought he was given special treatment by my parents and I was very jealous of him. He had a much bigger cupboard than I had, and his clothes always seemed less shabby than mine.

But worst of all, he had more money than I. It didn't take much detective work by me to discover that he kept it all in a piggy bank in his bedroom. One day, while he was out, I got hold of his money box and roughly shook out the coins.

To make my theft seem like an accident I then went around to the local police station.

'Sir,' I told the burly officer behind the desk, 'I found these coins in the street. What should I do?'

He scratched his chin, then his eyes lit up.

'Look, son, we have a law here in Holland that if anyone finds money in the street it becomes his after a year if nobody claims it.'

Soon I was regularly 'finding money in the street' and

pulling this trick. My patience in waiting for that year to elapse paid handsome dividends.

I had completely forgotten my 'crime' till it came flooding back to me at that meeting.

I felt the Lord saying to me, 'Andrew, you cannot get more from me unless you first confess your sin.'

So later, back in my room at the college, I penned a letter to Ben admitting my thefts and asking him to forgive me.

'Of course I am going to pay back to you everything I stole,' I told him.

A short time later, I received a most moving letter back from him.

'Andrew,' he said, 'there is nothing to forgive or pay back; the only debt we have to each other is to love each other.'

At that same meeting, God also reminded me of a time during the war when I had stolen apples. I would go to a large wholesaler near my home where thousands of crates of apples were stored. Because I couldn't get the complete apples out, I would slice pieces off with my pocket knife and eat them.

The next time I was in Holland I went back to the farm and confessed my wartime thievery to the owner.

'Sir, I've become a Christian and I know what I did was wrong. I would like to pay you back ten times the value of those apples I spoiled.'

He shook his head in disbelief. 'Oh my,' he said. 'I have never heard of this kind of thing before. Of course I won't accept the payment from you. But what you have told me is a good witness to the God you follow. Thank you for coming.'

I then returned to a shop where, when I was about twelve years old, I had stolen cigarette lighters and pocket knives, one of which I'd used to cut out those apples.

'Here, please take this money to pay for those things I took all that time back,' I told the bemused owner.

He gratefully took the cash and commented, 'If everybody would do that for what has been stolen from here over the years, I could close the shop and become a millionaire.'

I had done wrong as a child and then put it right and confessed and made reparation. It was a wonderful experience. And it certainly brought me closer to the Lord.

7: Masses of marching youth

IT was Spring 1955 and my two years at the W.E.C. Missionary Training College were about to come to an end. As graduation approached I felt more and more uneasy. So I decided to go and see Stewart Dinnen, the director of studies, and make a strange request of him.

'Mr Dinnen, I would very much appreciate it if I wasn't awarded a diploma from the college . . .'

His mouth fell agape and he shifted uncomfortably in his chair.

'You see, sir, I don't want any missionary society to take me into service just because I have a diploma from a Bible school. I want to follow the Lord and only do his will.'

Mr Dinnen chuckled in surprise.

'If that's what you want, Andrew,' he finally responded, 'that's great. It will certainly save me three minutes of writing it out.'

I thought he could have been a little more tactful, but thanked him all the same. So with that little action, I made W.E.C. history. I was the first student to leave that school without a diploma.

But now I had got over that hurdle, I had to turn my attention to what I should do. Where should I go?

My friend Kees was already in Korea and kept writing to me telling me the needs and opportunities in that war-devastated land.

As I was searching for God's guidance, I happened to pick up a magazine that changed my life. Just seven days before I was to leave, I went down to the musty basement of the college to collect my suitcase. As I sorted through the cobweb-covered cases and cardboard boxes reeking of mildew in that dank cellar, I came across a magazine on top of one of the boxes.

I began casually flicking through the pages. It certainly was well produced, printed as it was on glossy paper and packed with full-colour pictures of masses of marching youths parading on the streets of Warsaw and Peking and Prague.

'These young people are part of a worldwide organisation ninety-six million strong . . .' declared part of the text.

I was intrigued. Who were these people? What were they marching for? How was it I hadn't been taught about them in Bible school? Then I noticed that towards the back of the magazine, there was an announcement of a youth festival to be held in Warsaw, Poland, that coming July.

'Everyone is invited!' said the magazine.

EVERYONE!

That night I wrote to the Warsaw address mentioned in the magazine.

> 'Dear Sir,
>
> I am training to be a Christian missionary, and would like to come to the youth festival to exchange ideas: I would like to talk about Jesus Christ, and listen to others talk about socialism. Is it possible for me to come under those circumstances?'

I popped it through one of those sturdy red British letter boxes, a prayer on my lips.

Soon a reply came back saying it would be perfectly acceptable for me to come under those circumstances.

'Since you are a student,' said the writer, 'you can have reduced rates. A special train is leaving from Amsterdam so we look forward to seeing you soon in Warsaw.'

'Thank you, Lord. I now know you want me to go!'

After a brief stay back in Witte, I was off for my trip of a lifetime. The train for Warsaw left Amsterdam on July 15, 1955. I was amazed to see the hordes of students also going to the festival. Hundreds of bright-eyed young men and women filled the station.

I could hardly carry my suitcase. It was so heavy. I had packed it with just a few clothes – a change of linen and some extra socks. Most of the case was filled with small thirty-one page booklets called *The Way of Salvation*. I had been led to this festival by a piece of literature and so I was going to use literature to try and attract those also attending to come to Jesus Christ.

I knew that Karl Marx had once said, 'Give me twenty-six lead soldiers and I will conquer the world.' He was, of course, referring to the twenty-six letters of the alphabet in a fount of printing type. I realised that we, as Christians, were in a war of words. So I was going to play the Communists at their own game I was going to Poland with editions of this powerful little book in many European languages.

Once in the Polish capital, I was assigned to my 'hotel' which turned out to be a school building that had been converted into dormitories especially for the festival.

'We have arranged special sightseeing tours for you,' announced the attractive lady who was assigned to be our guide for the three weeks, 'and then in the afternoon and evenings you will listen to inspiring speeches about the great changes that socialism has made in building a new order.'

One morning I decided that I had heard enough of the claims of these speakers. I wanted to see for myself how they stood up to close scrutiny, at least in Warsaw. I wanted to peel back the well-scrubbed face of Warsaw and see what lay behind the façade. We had been shown a succession of new schools, factories, high-rise blocks of flats, and shops full of food and material goods. But was there more to see?

Before the rest of the group were down for breakfast, I darted out of the building. I gulped deeply at the mild morning air. But soon my mouth fell open in shock as I stumbled across sights the official guide had not shown us. I saw whole blocks that had been reduced to rubble by World War Two. Here, ten years after it had ended, were slum areas worse than anything I had ever seen, with long food queues of men and women dressed in rags. What had the great revolution done for these starving people? Why did they still not have decent homes?

One area into which I ventured provided me with a scene that is forever etched into my memory. I came to a bombed-out street and discovered that families there were living like rabbits in a warren. They had dug their way into the basements and were making their homes in them. I smiled at one little girl – she looked like a rag doll – who was playing barefoot amid the dust and debris.

'Hey, little girl, I want to give you something.'

I held out in my hand a Polish book and handed it to her. She snatched it from my hand and scurried up the mound of rubble. Moments later a woman dressed in filthy rags emerged with a man. Both were rip-roaring drunk. Both had despairing pouches of weariness under their eyes.

I tried to tell them that I wanted them to read the booklet.

They just gazed uncomprehendingly at me. Then it occurred to me that they couldn't read.

When I got back to the 'hotel' I shared a table with Hans, a Dutch communist. He told me how enthusiastic he was about what he had seen and heard. He couldn't understand why I was not.

'Hans, why don't you skip tomorrow's guided tour and go on your own,' I asked him. 'Go into the main street, turn left and then you will see some heaps of rubble. Go close to the rubble and you will find an opening; go in and you will find people there. Talk to them and see if they consider this to be a paradise on earth.'

Hans looked at me in pained surprise and shook his head. Surely he hadn't been taken in? He was a thinking Dutchman. To his credit, Hans did go out and enquire for himself. He went into the slum areas on his own, into the festering ruins where the people 'lived'.

That evening I saw Hans again. He looked pale and frightened. 'Andrew, I'm leaving tonight on the midnight train. I am scared stiff by what I have seen and heard today.'

The 'thinking Dutchman' had at last seen what I had, and had begun to think.

'I am sure no one else in 30,000 visitors to the city has seen what you have today, Hans. The problem is they are not prepared to ask questions. They only want to be on the guided tour and see nice things. There's lots of people like that.'

On that first Sunday I decided to visit a Baptist church in Warsaw and when word spread to the pastor that there was a foreigner in the congregation, he invited me to the front to speak.

It was an incredible experience to be able to share the Gospel in a Communist country. But even more moving was what the pastor said at the end of my talk.

He looked at me, his eyes shining, and said, 'Andrew, we want to thank you for *being* here. Even if you had not said a word, just seeing you would have meant so much. We feel at times as if we are *all alone* in our struggle.'

During that trip I also visited a Bible store in Warsaw. After observing the few people who trickled in, I waited for the shop to empty of customers. Then I asked the proprietor if there were Bible bookshops in other Communist countries.

He looked at me in a non-committal way and shrugged,

'Some yes, some no.' Obviously embarrassed he turned his back on me and began dusting the shelves.

Then he half-muttered, 'I understand that in Russia Bibles are very scarce indeed. In fact fortunes are being made there.'

I was by now most interested in what he was saying.

'A man smuggles ten Bibles into Russia and sells them for enough to buy a motor-cycle. He drives the motorcycle back into Poland or Yugoslavia or East Germany and sells it for a fat profit, with which he buys more Bibles.'

That story really hit me. He smuggled the Bibles for profit! I wondered if anyone was smuggling the Scriptures into the Soviet Union for love . . . the love of Jesus.

★　★　★

The climax of my visit was the Parade of Triumph. I stood on the side of one of Warsaw's wide avenues and watched thousands of young people marching towards me. They were martial, smart, and sang songs at the tops of their voices in praise of Marxism. They marched eight abreast, a tremendous advertisement for socialism.

As these clean-cut young men and women came past me I realised that they were the evangelists of the twentieth century. They believed they had good news for the world and were not ashamed to shout it out.

I also realised that part of their 'good news' was that man was his own master; the future was in his hands. Religion was part of the old superstitions and had to go. There was no further need for it.

As many thoughts whirled around in my head, I eased my Bible out of my pocket in that vast crowd. The pages fluttered in the morning breeze and stopped at chapter three in the book of Revelation. Suddenly a verse came bounding off the page. It read: 'Awake and strengthen what remains and is on the point of death . . .'

I felt a tear begin to trickle down my face.

'Lord,' I asked, 'are you telling me that my life's work is to be here behind the Iron Curtain, where what is left of your Church is desperately struggling for its life?'

'Do you want me to play my part in strengthening this precious thing that remains?'

I tried to dismiss such a crazy idea from my thoughts. After all, back then in 1955, I had never even heard of so much as one missionary working in this huge mission field.

'Lord this is crazy,' I protested. 'What can one man do against such overwhelming odds? I see before me a force so strong and powerful that I feel I can do nothing.'

As I continued to resist, I felt the Lord saying quietly to me, 'Andrew, just be obedient. Leave the details to me.'

I smiled and slipped my Bible back into my pocket.

I was beginning to 'Awake' myself to a whole new world . . . trapped behind barbed wire.

8: The cup of suffering

ANGER was written all over her face.

'I didn't like what you said,' she snapped, wagging an admonishing finger at me. I recognised the lady with short-cropped hair as the leader of the Dutch delegation in Warsaw. She had just sat stone-faced through a talk I had given at a church in Haarlem about my findings during that eye-opening visit to Poland.

'You only told part of the story,' she continued, her voice filled with rancour. 'You obviously haven't seen enough. You need to travel more, visit more socialist countries, meet more leaders.'

I didn't make any comment, but she dumbfounded me when she added, 'In other words, you ought to take another trip, and that's what I've come to suggest.'

She revealed that she was in charge of selecting fifteen people from Holland to take a trip to Czechoslovakia. The visit would last two weeks, and in the group there would be students and professors and people in communications.

'We'd like someone from the churches,' she added. 'Would you come?'

I looked blankly at her and then quickly offered up a silent prayer to the Lord saying that if he wanted me to go then he would have to supply the funds.

Then I turned to her. 'I am flattered that you would like me to come, but I could never afford such a trip. I'm really sorry.'

She stared even more intently at me. 'Well, we can work

that out. For you, there will be no charge.'

So this was how my second trip behind the Iron Curtain began. The group was smaller than the one with which I went to Poland so I encountered much more trouble in skipping official tours.

'Lord, why am I here?' I prayed near the end of the four weeks. All I am seeing is in praise of the "great" revolution.'

'Andrew,' said the Czech tour guide one day, 'I know you are interested in religion in my country. Well we have great freedom here.

'Look, there are even a group of scholars being paid by our government to bring out a new translation of the Bible. They are also working on a Bible dictionary.'

I was amazed and asked if I could visit these men.

That afternoon I went to the Interchurch Centre, head-quarters for all Protestant churches in Czechoslovakia. The centre was housed in a large office building in the centre of Prague.

I was taken by the guide through a labyrinth of cramped and old-fashioned offices until I came to some rooms inhabited by scholarly looking gentlemen resplendent in black coats. They seemed to be buried under disorganised piles of paper and large books.

'Can I see a copy of the new translation?' I asked after hearing that these were the men who had actually worked on the project. I was passed a large, much-handled manuscript.

'No, I meant the actual Bible . . .'

The man who had handed it to me, looked sad.

'I'm afraid you can't . . .' He hesitated for a moment and then added, 'we've had it ready since the war, but . . .'

He then told me that the Bible dictionary was almost ready, but I could see that it would be of no use if there were no Bibles.

The translator, a map of wrinkles covering his sad face,

stared at the tour director, wondering whether or not to say any more. He finally blurted out, 'It's very difficult. Very difficult to find Bibles here nowadays.'

'Well . . . thank you, sir, I must take my Dutch friend away now.' I was whisked away by the director without being able to ask any more questions.

However, I had been able to grasp the game the Communist government was playing. Rather than openly attacking the Church, it was frustrating its efforts. The Government was sponsoring a Bible translation, but delaying its release.

Next day I went with the tour director to the Interdenominational Book Store. Surely they would have Bibles here? The shop was overflowing with stationery, pictures, statues, crosses, music and books that had some connection with religion.

But Bibles were not easy to come by. I asked to buy several versions but was told that none of them was available at that time.

Finally, the manager, on hearing I was from Holland, managed to unearth one Bible from a storeroom at the back of the shop and handed it me. It was already wrapped in brown paper, as if he didn't want anyone to know what was inside.

I thanked him warmly and he explained, 'It's the new translation that makes Bibles scarce. Until that comes out, new Bibles just aren't being printed.'

* * *

It seemed to me as if everyone in the congregation of that Prague church was longsighted. As I sat in the back, I noticed that the owners of hymn books held them out high in the air. There were also notebooks held up at arm's length. It was then I realised that in these notebooks were copied the favourite hymns of the church.

When the preacher announced the texts, those who owned Bibles found them and held their books high so that those around could also follow the reading. As I held my own Dutch Bible I realised how much I had taken for granted the fact that I was freely able to own a copy of this great Book.

On that last day of my visit, a Sunday, I had managed to escape from the organised activities by slipping out the rear door of the tour bus when it stopped at a red light. It was an area of Prague where I knew the church was. I knew the director would be hopping mad, but I just had to make some investigations without her at my side checking that I was told all the right things.

As the preacher came to the back to shake hands with the congregation at the end of the service, I stood at his side.

'Brother,' I said quietly, 'I am a believer from Holland. I am here to meet with Christians in your country.

I saw a little tear begin to trickle down his face.

'Brother,' he said, his voice quivering with emotion, 'please come and talk to me. We have almost been imprisoned here since the war. You are the first believer to come from the West for many years.'

At his flat he told me how dangerous it was to be a Christian leader in the Czechoslovakia of 1955.

'The government is trying to get a stranglehold on the Church,' he confided. 'They are even choosing the theological students – only those who support the regime get places.

'Do you know that every two months I have to renew my licence? This happens with all pastors. A friend of mine recently had his request turned down. They didn't tell him why. They don't have to.'

But surely he was free to preach what he wished?

'No, that is not true, my friend,' he said as he lowered his eyes. 'We have to write out a sermon ahead of time and it has to be approved by the authorities.'

I whistled.

'Now, my brother, we are going to have another service. I'd like you to come and speak to us.'

I was taken aback.

'But,' I pointed out, 'I thought sermons had to be submitted for checking.'

'No, I am not asking you to *preach*. But I want you to bring "greetings" from our brothers and sisters in your country.'

His face creased into a broad grin. 'And if you wished to, you could also bring us "greetings" from the Lord.'

Through an interpreter, a young medical student called Antonin, I brought brief greetings from my homeland and also 'the West'. Then I took thirty minutes to bring greetings 'from Jesus Christ' to the congregation. My interpreter felt that this was such a wonderful new device that I should try it again at another church . . . and another . . . and another . . . until at the end of the day I had preached five times at five different churches.

It was now getting late on that November day, and I felt I should be getting back to the hotel. I guessed the tour leader would soon be sending out a search party for me.

But then Antonin asked if I would go to one more church. So we went across Prague until we arrived at the tiny Moravian church. There about forty young people aged between eighteen and twenty-five packed into the room. After I had brought 'greetings' they bombarded me with questions. They were astonished when I told them that you were not reported to the government in Holland for going to church, or that you could attend church and still be allowed to go to a good university.

Antonin explained that a Christian believer in Czechoslovakia was looked upon as unpatriotic. 'Many of these young people have been forced out of jobs and have missed out on education because of their stand for Christ,' he said.

He took out a small cardboard box from the outstretched hands of a young man at his side. 'They want you to have this gift of remembrance,' he explained.

Then, with Antonin interpreting, the young man asked me to take it back to Holland. 'Brother, when people there ask you about it, tell them about us and remind them that we are part of the Body, too, and that we are in pain.'

I gently opened the book and lifted out a silver lapel ornament in the shape of a small cup.

'Many of those here are wearing them. What are they?' I queried to Antonin.

He took it from me and pinned it on my jacket. 'This,' he said, 'is the symbol of the Church in Czechoslovakia. We call it the Cup of Suffering.

'You are now a partaker of that cup!'

9: The smuggler's prayer

'MR Whestra, I'm going behind the Iron Curtain as a missionary! What do you think?'

I waited for his purr of pleasure down the telephone line. Instead, he changed the subject and told me that I should come home from West Berlin, from where I was phoning, to collect 'your keys'.

What was he talking about?

'It's the keys to your Volkswagen,' he said as my jaw dropped in unfeigned surprise. 'Mrs Whestra decided that if you got a visa for your next trip to Yugoslavia, you also got our car. Come home and collect the keys.'

When I got to their house no amount of protesting on my part could talk them out of giving me such a large gift.

'Andrew,' said Mr Whestra firmly, 'you are now in the King's business! No, we've prayed about it, and these are our orders.'

So with that I became the owner of a shiny blue, almost new Volkswagen.

It wasn't long before I was at the Yugoslav border with the new vehicle. My luggage was packed full of tracts, Bibles, and Scripture portions. At that time in 1957, the Yugoslav government only allowed visitors to bring in items for their personal use. I had been warned by a well-travelled friend that printed material was definitely liable to be confiscated at the border, no matter how small the quantity.

'They regard it as propaganda,' my friend gravely explained.

I was in a tiny Austrian village near the Yugoslavian border, when I first uttered what I now call the 'Smuggler's Prayer'.

As I sat at the wheel, I closed my eyes and said, 'Lord in my luggage I have Scriptures that I want to take to your children across this border. When you were on earth, you made blind eyes see. Now, I pray, make seeing eyes blind. Do not let the guards see those things you do not want them to see.'

I had decided right at the beginning that I would never tell a lie to a border guard. But I also determined to pray mighty hard that I didn't have to tell the truth either!

The two border guards seemed glad to have me there.

'It's very quiet here these days,' one of them smiled as he began to examine my documents. His colleague busied himself by feeling around in my camping items and was coming dangerously close to finding the boxes of tracts I had packed in the folds of my sleeping bag and tent.

'Lord,' I whispered urgently, 'please make seeing eyes blind.'

The first uniformed guard asked if I had anything to declare.

'Well,' I began. 'I have money, my wristwatch and my camera.'

'Anything else?'

'Only "small things",' I said as convincingly as I could. The tracts were, after all, small.

'We don't need to bother with them,' he said as he nodded, saluted, and gave me back my passport.

The whole trip was like a dream come true. For seven weeks I was able to preach, teach, encourage, and personally hand to grateful believers the Scriptures I had brought. In those fifty days I held more than eighty meetings. Some Sundays I spoke as many as six times. In the north of the country I was able to speak openly, but in the south, where the Communist influence was stronger, I had to be more careful.

I discovered that the tactics of the Yugoslav government were to leave the older people alone, but work on the children in a bid to warn them away from the Church.

'We are taught in school that there is no God,' explained one young student.

I learned of Marta, a young Christian girl who always said grace before meals at home. At school she continued the practice, and gave thanks aloud for her food. She was expelled for doing this. 'You will fill the other children's minds with nonsense,' she was told.

As I bounced along the roads of Yugoslavia I realised how easy it would be for the V.W. to seize up. Dust lay thickly over the unpaved highways and so each morning I would pray with Nikola, a Yugoslav believer who was acting as my interpreter, that he would keep the car mobile as I didn't have the time or the money for repairs on the vehicle.

I usually mentioned this story during my meetings and it always brought laughter and applause from the congregation.

As I was travelling one day towards Terna, I spotted a small lorry coming the other way. It was the custom in those days that if you had a foreign car you would stop to have a brief chat with the driver going the other way. You would swap information about road conditions, the weather, and the possibility of buying petrol.

Aleksander, this driver, was particularly friendly.

'You are Brother Andrew, aren't you?' Before I could reply, he pointed to my car.

'And this,' he continued, 'is the "Miracle Car"?'

I nodded.

'Do you mind if I look at her? I'm a mechanic.' He lifted

the bonnet and began checking over the engine. Soon he was scratching his head. Then he turned to me and explained that it was 'mechanically impossible' for this car to run. He said that the carburetor was clogged, as was the air filter. The sparking plugs were coked.

Aleksander asked if he could tune up the engine for me and give it a change of oil.

'It hurts to see you abuse a miracle . . .' he told me.

* * *

May Day, 1957, saw Belgrade packed to capacity. This high holy day of Communism had brought in people from all over the country.

As many later drank the night away, I was in a church that was so full that I felt as if we were sardines pressed inside a tin. I was illustrating my stories of the Gospel with a flannel-graph when I suddenly heard the sound of hammering.

I jumped, thinking the Secret Police were coming in to arrest me. Somehow I continued talking, and as I did the door was suddenly lifted right off its hinges. It was only then that I realised that this was being done to allow the overflow of people in the next room to hear.

After spending so much time in the countryside, I found it a fascinating contrast to be in a church with a more sophisticated congregation, well-dressed, well-educated.

At the end of the talk, I told everyone that I was going to give them a chance to accept Jesus Christ as their Saviour or to recommit their lives to Christ.

'If you are willing to take either of these steps, I want you to raise your hand,' I explained.

Suddenly there was a sea of hands pointing upwards.

'Look, I think you have misunderstood me,' I said. 'You know all too well the cost of following Jesus in this country. I am not offering you an easy life. All that I can offer you is a Cup of Suffering . . .'

I asked them this time to stand up if they really wanted to make a commitment. Everyone stood up!

I was amazed, so I began to tell those who just became Christians for the first time about the importance of prayer and daily Bible study. For some unknown reason I sensed a great embarrassment in the congregation.

'What's the problem?' I asked the pastor.

He, too, seemed ill at ease.

'Andrew,' he said through Nikola, 'we can pray each day. I like what you have said about this. But Bible reading . . . Brother Andrew, most of these people do not have Bibles.'

I was shocked. I had expected the people in the rural areas to be short of the Scriptures, but not in this great city of Belgrade.

'How many of you own Bibles?' I finally asked the congregation.

Only seven hands went up, and that included the pastor. I felt helpless. I had already handed out the Bibles I had brought through the border with me. What could I give these people who were taking a conscious step to swim against the rising tide of atheistic communism in their country?

After the service, I sat with the pastor and we worked out a plan of Bible-sharing, so that each member could have the loan of a Bible at least for a few hours. That night in bed in the pastor's room I began talking to the Lord.

'Lord, I pledge to you right now that I will give over the rest of my life to bring in your Word to these, your children caught behind this man-made Iron Curtain.

'Whatever doors you open up for me, I'll walk through them . . . armed of course with your Word and protection.'

★ ★ ★

Although most of my time over the next few years was to be taken up with 'smuggling' Bibles into Eastern Europe, there was one occasion when I brought out a load of Bibles in Eastern European languages so they could be repacked in Holland and taken in later. I had visited West Berlin, and was heading back home through the hundred mile Russian-occupied zone of East Germany to West Germany. I had been working in refugee camps there with Dutch theologian Anton, and we had been giving out Scriptures to the people from different countries and languages. I had a load of Bibles left in Eastern European languages which I was taking back with me to Holland where I could repack them, and later take them myself or send them or have other teams take them to the Eastern European countries.

I had not hidden them. I just had them all in cardboard boxes because so far I had never encountered any problems at the East German border between Berlin and West Germany. This time as I stopped there at Helmstadt, an officer came up to my car and pointed to one of the cardboard boxes.

'What's in there?'

With a very big smile, I said, 'Sir, there are Bibles in that box.'

He frowned.

'Take the box into my office,' he ordered.

We did. We carried the heavy box into his office and put all the books on tables. We filled three tables with New Testaments, Gospels, and complete Bibles in various Eastern European languages, including German.

He checked every book to see where it was printed.

Fortunately they weren't printed in New York; they were all from Sweden, Germany, Switzerland and Holland, so we passed these.

'Do you have anything else?' he asked.

Again I smiled, and said, 'Yes, sir. I have a lot more.'

He marched back to my vehicle, right to the back of the V.W., and pointed to a box.

'What's in there?'

'Flannelgraph stories.'

'What are they?'

I have developed a habit of making very long sentences, in order to get the Gospel across in every sentence. A guard has to listen to at least one sentence if he asks me a question! That way I can tell about Jesus.

'Well, sir,' I responded, 'they are flannelgraph stories that teachers use to tell children about the Lord Jesus Christ, because even children can believe on him, because when a child is old enough to love his parents he can love Jesus who came into the world to save sinners so that children as well as grown-up people by simple faith in him can have eternal life and go to heaven when they die.'

That was my sermonette in a sentence.

He left the box right there, but he pulled out one of the folders and opened it in my car. I was embarrassed because it was a map of the Mediterranean with the travels of the Apostle Paul marked with dots and lines, and all the countries, seas, and islands identified. It looked like a spy map!

He seemed very cross. 'Aha! You said it was for little children . . .'

'Yes, sir,' I interrupted, 'this is just a map of the travels of the Apostle Paul who first of all came to Europe to tell about the Lord Jesus Christ so that we in Europe should hear about the great message of Jesus Christ, and if he had not come here we would still be barbarians living without God – practically as atheists.'

That was my second sermonette.

He really got mad with me then.

'Take it into my office!'

We did. The office was full of 'Red' soldiers picking up those beautiful books, trying to read the Word of God. When I put the box down, more people flowed into that hall – mainly East German soldiers and officers.

The officer pulled another folder from my box – and again, it was the worst possible one he could have chosen. It was the story of Ephesians 6, and how we need to take on the whole armour of God! When he opened it, out fell the cardboard sword and the helmet and all the rest. It looked very dangerous for me.

Again there was that angry look on his face.

'I thought this was for children,' he snapped.

'Really, it is!' I insisted. 'I can't explain it, but let me demonstrate it.'

I asked my friend Anton to hold the background of black cloth. He was tall, 6'2", and held it back against the wall. I took a figure of an undressed boy and stuck it to the flannelgraph background to tell the story.

'Here is a man in the world, unprotected from sin and demons and sickness and darkness and disease. He needs protection. Man cannot live without God . . .'

I put the helmet of salvation on him.

'You've got to believe in the Lord Jesus Christ to be saved and know that you have eternal life.'

Then I quickly put on the breastplate of righteousness.

'Because you have to live a righteous life, and all these godless people in this world make a mess of it and murder people . . .' I gave the story, of course, about Hitler's Nazi Germany. '. . . and now we can't allow that to happen because people living without God bring the whole world into bondage.'

Then I put the shield of faith in the little figure's hand and said that with faith we are protected. 'Whatever happens in the world, if we have personal faith through salvation in our hearts, we live a holy life and we have the shield of faith so that all the onslaughts of the enemy, all the attacks can be thwarted right here with the shield of faith . . .'

I was just going to grab the sword and put it in his hand and speak about the Word of God, when it dawned on the man that I was preaching to them! Well, I had a captive audience – the office was filled with soldiers and officers – and of course I spoke in German. When he found out that I was preaching, he was furious.

'Now stop this! Put it all back in your boxes and take it to your car and go!'

'No, sir,' I said. 'I would like to give each of you a souvenir. I somewhat enjoyed being with you so long.'

I got out a pile of John's Gospels and tried to hand them ouut. They couldn't possibly accept them. They put their hands behind their backs and marched away, leaving Anton and me to take the Bibles and flannelgraph stories back to the car – and we drove away!

God had allowed us to hold a unique gospel meeting.

But we had only gone a short way when a soldier stepped out from the side of the road and frantically flagged us down. We looked at each other, feeling that they had only let us go for a joke. Actually now we were to be arrested.

I nervously wound down my window and waited for the soldier to speak.

'I am afraid you are in serious trouble,' he began.

I gulped and waited for the worst.

'Yes, you will be fined on the spot for speeding. You have just exceeded the limit of five kilometers per hour.'

He said that the instant fine would be the equivalent of £5 ($10 U.S.) and so we happily paid up.

With that he clicked his heels and signalled us to continue – but this time within the limit.

'I guess we can consider that the "offering" for our little service,' I chuckled once we were safely in West Germany.

'Yes,' laughed my companion. 'I guess that is a cheap offering for such a service.'

10: 'Will you marry me'

A FULL moon lit up the little track along which we were cycling. I now had a new girlfriend, Corry van Dam, a shy, pretty girl I had originally met when I was working in a chocolate factory.

Corry became the new girl in my life after I had received a shock letter from Thile which informed me that my decision to go to the W.E.C. college in Glasgow meant that we had to part.

Thile knew little about what were called 'faith missions' and had gone to see the heads of the mission department of her Reformed Church. They had advised her that the only way a person could be a missionary was through the Church. The believer had to go through their theological training, then become ordained.

Her letter had concluded: 'Andrew, I do know that both our hearts go out to the unreached people of the world, but the board assured me that you cannot do this work if you are not an ordained minister.

'I am fully aware of the long time this training will take – at least twelve years. If you were prepared to do this I would support and help you. But only if you would follow the line of the Church and then become a missionary.

'But since you have chosen W.E.C. and are already in training for this so-called "faith mission" I feel I have to follow the advice of the council mission leaders and that means we will not see each other again.

'God bless you,

'Thile.'

I was so disappointed by her letter that I decided not even to reply to it, though I was sorely tempted to tell that there were many great Christians who had walked with God and yet didn't have a denomination or organisation behind them or even any regular salary.

So now I was with Corry. Our courtship had blossomed after Corry had made a pact with the Lord over boyfriends. She was over twenty-five years old and, like many young ladies of that age, had been getting more than a little concerned about the fact that she was not going out with a regular boyfriend. So she had begun attending youth services and camps in the hope of finding the right young man.

One Sunday morning, however, she felt convicted about the fact that she had been tring to manipulate the situation. So she sank to her knees and handed over her life completely to God.

'Lord,' she prayed earnestly, 'if you want me to have a boyfriend, you will have to bring him right into my home. I will not search any more.'

After that prayer, Corry felt an overwhelming peace flood her being. Just as she stood up, a knock came on the front door. She answered it and found that I was standing there.

In reply to the questioning look on her face, I explained, 'Corry, I've come to ask about your father. I hear he is ill.'

Wearing a crisp, white, nurse's uniform, she led me quietly to her father's room. I could see from the pallor on his face that he was gravely ill. He seemed pleased to have a visitor and so, for an hour, I shared with him news about my trips behind the Iron Curtain and my hopes for the future. Every few minutes, Corry would come into the room bearing bottles and trays.

Thus began our nervous courtship – at first a few

hushed conversations after my twice-weekly visits to Mr van Dam, till eventually we were head over heels in love. So now I was with Corry. Yet I knew that the kind of life I was living was not really the best recommendation for a future life together.

Finally, on that moonlit evening, I stopped pedalling and signalled her to come and sit with me at the side of the canal. It was an emotional time for her as her father had recently died.

'Corry,' I faltered, 'I want you to marry me, but don't say anything until I've told you how hard it will be. Hard for me and still harder for you.'

She looked at me, eyes sparkling, but said nothing.

'I haven't told you all that I've been doing recently. On my last trip into Eastern Europe I travelled nearly six thousand miles in the seven weeks I was away.'

She clasped my hand as the colour rose up in her cheeks.

'But you haven't told me what you did while you were there, Andrew.'

'Well, I held almost one hundred meetings and saw hundreds of new Christians born into God's Kingdom,' I said. 'It was a wonderful experience . . .'

Then I returned to my strange proposal, and this time I really put my foot in it.

'Corry, you'd be crazy to marry me. But I do so want you to.' I wrapped my arm around her slender shoulders.

We both promised to do nothing until I had returned from my next visit to Eastern Europe, this time to Romania. It was a wonderful trip with God again making 'seeing eyes blind' and giving me new contacts.

Corry was working as a nurse in a hospital in Haarlem so, when I knew her late-night shift was concluding, I went straight there. She smiled with joy when she saw me waiting for her outside the large front door.

'You're safe, Andrew,' she said. 'I've been so worried for you.'

I took her hand and then kissed it.

'Corry, I love you . . . whether the answer is yes or no.'

She looked exhausted from another evening of back-breaking work. but her face creased into a shy smile and the tiredness seemed to melt away from her features.

'Andrew, I love you, too! Don't you see that's just the trouble? I'm going to worry about you, and miss you, and pray for you, no matter what. So hadn't I better be a worried *wife* than just a worried *friend?*'

Just a few days later we bought two wedding rings. Our Dutch custom is to wear the ring on the left hand during the engagement and transfer it to the right at the marriage ceremony. We carried the little boxes containing the rings up to her tiny sitting-room, and we knelt down by the side of the sofa and gently took them out. Still on our knees we placed them on each other's hands.

I looked tenderly at her and said, 'Corry, we don't know where the road leads, do we?'

She smiled and her eyes became even larger as she uttered for the first time the words that were to become our motto.

'But, Andrew, let's go there together.'

* * *

The Soviet Union was the next country on my agenda. And it was there that I met a Russian Christian who made a deep impression on me. Joseph told me that he had been in a labour camp for ten years for his faith. As we talked, he revealed that, while in the camp, he had made a most unusual Bible.

'Andrew,' he said, 'my job in the camp was to empty cement bags. I had managed to get hold of a pencil and I would rip off pieces of the thick brown bags and write on them the Bible verses I could remember.

'I managed to fill twelve pages with these verses and often, when I was alone in a quiet corner, I would be joined by other Christians. Then I would open my shirt and pull out the "cement-bag Bible" hidden under it and we would read the verses together.

'How I loved that Bible,' he told me as his eyes filled with tears.

He then produced the clandestine Holy Book for me to see.

'My brother,' I asked him, 'may I have it in my hand just for a moment?'

He agreed to my request and I almost wept. What a love this believer had for his cement-bag Bible. I wished that I had that much love for my Bible.

In that great land I also met the man who never said 'thank you'.

I came across him near the end of my trip all over Russia. I had by now graduated from the faithful blue Volkswagen to a much larger station wagon, in which I could carry hundreds of Bibles at one time. As the work had progressed, so had the support I received and I was able to get more and more Scriptures through unfriendly borders. Now, on this journey, I only had one of those contraband Scriptures left.

I entered the last church on my itinerary and found it absolutely packed to the doors. It was a warm summer's day and all the windows were open. That meant that the 'overflow' could gather by these windows to listen outside.

For more than an hour, as the large congregation hung on to his every word, the pastor preached a stirring sermon. Many had tears trickling down their cheeks as they learned more of God's love for them.

After closing in prayer, the pastor signalled for me to

follow him into a little bare vestry. Some twelve elders followed us in.

'Brother Andrew,' he said, knowing that I would weave a Bible study into my greetings, 'would you please bring us "greetings" from Holland?'

I smiled, picked up my black leather-bound Bible and passed on what the Lord had laid on my heart for the little group for a further thirty minutes.

The pastor interpreted for me and, as I sat down again, I noticed that he was fondly gazing at my Bible with its beautiful print and leather cover.

He picked it up from the table where I had left it and held it close to his heart with an affection I have never seen in a Western Christian.

'Brother,' he said sadly as he returned it to the table. 'I have no Bible.'

I was stunned. He had preached to a big crowd without a Bible and I had not even noticed. This man was a great evangelist and teacher – yet he had no tools to work with.

'Please wait a minute pastor; I will be right back,' I said as I bounded out to my car to bring back the one Russian Bible I had with me. It was a pocket-sized version I had been presented with in the Ukraine. I had planned to take it back to Holland with me to show the Bible Society to see if they could publish thousands of them for me.

'Well, I guess they'll just have to take my word for the fact that they exist,' I muttered quietly.

I turned to him and pressed the Bible into his hands.

'It's yours, dear brother. Please take it.' He just stood still and gazed at it. He never said, 'Thank you'. He was dumb-struck. It was as if I had given him a million roubles.

'Brother Andrew, I have never owned a Bible in my whole life,' he said, trying to choke back the tears. It was one of the most moving moments I have ever experienced.

When I got home to my wife Corry I shared with her the great need for pocket Bibles.

'We can take so many more in if they are small,' I enthused.

But Corry as practical as ever, asked where the money was coming from to pay for them.

It was then 1963 and I had calculated that it would cost around £7,500 ($15,000 U.S.) to get them printed. I had begun a bank account to pray for this project, but all I had left in it at that time was £1,000 ($2,000 U.S.).

So I sat down with my wife, who was expecting a baby, and talked over the value of our house. We loved the place, yet its sale seemed to be the only way I could raise the necessary cash for the pocket Bibles.

All the colour drained from Corry's face when I first brought up the possibility of selling it.

'Maybe God doesn't want us to have those pocket Bibles,' she said, her voice almost inaudible. 'Maybe the slowness of the money coming in is his guidance.'

Despite this, Corry began to pray that she would think of the house not as her own, but belonging to God.

'It should be yours to do as you will,' we began praying that evening, 'and yet we know we really don't feel this way, Lord. If you want us to sell the house for the Bibles, you will have to work a small miracle in our hearts to make us willing.'

The baby was born. Cash gifts came in for our child, and we dutifully put it into the Pocket Bibles fund. But Corry and I knew that even if we continued saving for the next twenty years, at that present rate it would still not be enough. Finally we stopped asking for willingness and just asked to make us *willing* to be *willing* to let go of the house.

One day Corry came into my little office and held my hand.

'Andrew, we both know that we really don't need the house or any other material possession to make us happy as husband and wife.

'I don't know where we'll live. Remember, Andrew? We don't know where we're going . . .'

'But we're going there together,' I laughed.

Immediately, we got our house appraised, and the total, along with our savings account, came to just over £7,500. The breakthrough had come. Our beloved house was put up for sale and I made contact with the Bible Society to tell them of the great need for these small Russian Bibles. Corry and I were also happy because we had finally let go of 'our' house and made it 'his' house.

Despite the fact that there was an acute housing shortage in our village, no one came to view the property. It didn't seem to make sense. Then one afternoon a phone call came in from one leader of the Bible Society, requesting me to visit their office. I was moved as I was told that they would pay for the entire printing of the pocket Bibles, and I only needed to pay for my own supplies.

When I returned home, I hugged Corry and told her: 'Praise the Lord. We don't have to sell the house.' Naturally, she was delighted. The Lord honoured our willingness to sell, for the Russian pocket Bible became an absolute best-seller.

And the house? We stayed in it for another eight years.

11: Behind the sugarcane curtain

IT was certainly the strangest 'Cathedral' I'd ever been to. Set in a clearing on the edge of the Puerto Rican capital of San Juan, 'Catacomba Cathedral 1', was really just a clearing in a wood with tree stumps for seats.

I had been asked to speak to a group of Christians called the Catacombas, who are among the most unusual believers I have come across anywhere in the world.

'You know, Brother Andrew,' explained Pedro, the founder of this dedicated group, 'we don't believe in expensive buildings. We know that Jesus is coming back soon and we don't have the time to put them up. We need to use our time to tell others in our country about Jesus.'

He could see my intense interest, so explained that the movement began in 1971 after he had become a Christian.

'Before that I was taking LSD and hashish. My life was a real mess. I found that the churches in my country didn't seem too interested in people like me.

'Soon many others, mostly hippies, also came to know the Lord and we began meeting in what we humorously called "Catacomba Cathedral 1". We now have eighteen of these open-air meeting places around the island.'

But why the title Catacombas? I was perplexed.

'Oh,' he explained, 'we took that after I had read a book about martyred Christians and realised that one day we, too, could be called to lay down our lives for Christ.'

Pedro went on to say that the book spoke about the Catacombs of Rome, those subterranean vaults and passages constructed by the early Christians as a place of refuge during times of persecution.

As we talked, the Catacombas began singing at the top of their voices to the accompaniment of maracas, tambourines and guitars.

Pedro then introduced me to Manuel, another young Catacomba, who, after much hand-pumping, produced from the boot of his car a map which he unrolled.

'This,' he explained, 'is a map of the drain system of San Juan. You see, if persecution comes we can literally go underground immediately, just like the early Christians in Rome.

'We already have haversacks, sleeping bags, flashlights and military boots. We are prepared to go into hiding either in the drains or in the mountains.

'We even know of caves where we can hide Bibles.'

Pedro then came back into the conversation.

'We have already seen what has happened in Cuba,' he said with a deep conviction in his voice. 'Now Nicaragua has had its revolution and El Salvador is in the middle of its. We can see all these troubles creeping towards Puerto Rica.

'That's why we must prepare. We are willing to pay any price to keep our liberty as Christians. We know that persecution can come from either the left or the right.'

His face had become very serious.

'My friends,' he announced firmly, 'we are willing to be martyrs if God calls on us to be.'

When Pedro spoke of Cuba I knew from firsthand experience the truth of what he said. Back in 1965 I had gone behind Fidel Castro's 'Sugarcane Curtain' to make contact with believers there.

Not surprisingly, I was greeted with much suspicion by the Cuban authorities. After a short time in the country, I was asked to report to police headquarters – normal practice in any Communist country.

The police officer carefully examined my passport which clearly showed my visits to Russia, the United States and other nations. He wanted to know what I was doing in Cuba.

'I've come to preach the Gospel,' I told him honestly. That deepened his suspicions, and he grilled me for hours on end. For four days I was asked to report back for further questioning. And when it finally ended, I began to 'preach the Gospel'.

The Havana church where I was holding my meetings was a large one. Because so many at the church had come to know Christ, the authorities had mounted a campaign to make life difficult for the members. They had mobs gathering outside for each service, jostling and jeering those who went inside. Loudspeakers would blare out during the service, pavements would be torn up by noisy equipment and police would sit in the pews and take notes.

Yet, despite all that, thirty-five courageous Cubans came to the service to hear me on the first night. Next night, they all returned; on the following two nights sixty were there, soon it crept to over one hundred. I knew that some were 'policemen' so I was careful not to mention politics.

During one service I spoke on the subject outlined in John chapter 10; that a shepherd is not to leave his sheep or he becomes a hireling. When I had travelled before in Communist countries I had often met young people who wanted to leave their countries for the 'free' West, preferably the United States. I always said, 'Don't do it. If you know God, you should not flee. You must stay here and serve God, because you can only fight for God where there are his enemies. If you flee from the battlefield, if you shun the conflict, then you come into an area where you may not have the divine protection on your life any more.'

I had discovered that many of those who had left their countries had often lost their faith because of the materialistic society into which they had gone.

At the end of this sermon in Cuba, a well-groomed man, who turned out to be a pastor, stood up.

'Brother Andrew,' he told me in front of the hushed congregation, 'I have been planning to leave Cuba for America. My application papers are already being processed, but after what I have heard you say about a shepherd staying with the flock, I have decided before God tonight to stay.'

The people rose up as one and clapped their hands. They said, 'Gracias, Padre; O gracias, Padre.' They were so happy that this man was to stay. I heard later that he was greatly used of the Lord in Cuba, in that difficult situation.

At José Marti International Airport, Havana, a Cuban pastor came to see me off. As I started to go through immigration and customs, I felt I should ask him what he needed most.

He didn't hesitate.

'Brother Andrew, I need a pair of shoes.'

I grinned and then took mine off and handed them to him.

'Praise the Lord, brother! They are yours!' He took them gratefully. With that I padded through immigration and customs in my stockinged feet, and on to the plane.

As I clambered on to the jet, his last words kept ringing in my ears.

'Now you have given everything, Andrew. The only thing you have left to give is your life!'

The plane took us to Madrid and because there was a delay in the flight to Amsterdam, all of the passengers were taken into a first-class hotel in the Spanish capital. As I walked through the lobby in my socks I could see both staff and guests staring at me in amazement.

On a return visit to Cuba, I requested to see Fidel Castro, the man who has ruled the island since 1959 when he overthrew the hated dictator Batista. Many on this Caribbean island had turned Fidel into their God. But I wanted to share with him the real gospel.

However, the bearded revolutionary was too busy to give me an audience. Instead, I was allowed to see his Minister of Culture, who was then responsible for much of the persecution of the believers.

This man knew all about my previous activities on the island and looked sternly at me.

'Brother Andrew,' he said wagging his finger in my face, 'you are *not* to preach here any more.'

The minister had a large file in front of him listing details of where I had preached last time and with whom I had associated.

'But sir,' I countered, 'would you object if I asked questions of the people?'

He paused and rubbed his chin.

'Well . . . I can't see any objection in your doing that.'

With that concession under my belt I thought I would push open the door a little more.

'If people want to ask me questions, can I answer them?'

He paused a little longer, and then said, 'I suppose that would not cause any problems.'

I smiled gently, realising he was giving me carte blanche to continue my ministry on the island.

The more we talked, the more I realised that this man was completely dedicated to the Cuban revolution. He really believed that Karl Marx was right when he said that 'religion is the opiate of the masses.'

'Sir,' I held his gaze as I stated, 'if the Church in Russia had been truly Christian, there would never have been a revolution.'

He sat straight up in his chair. 'I agree,' he said, his eyes blazing. 'I don't have to tell you how pleased I am, Brother Andrew, that much of the Church of Jesus Christ worldwide is not truly Christian. Because of that, our revolution will continue to spread and nothing will stop it.

'We have one aim – to win this world. But you people often seem more concerned with pie in the sky.'

I knew there was a lot of truth in what he said.

'I can only respect a Christian if he tries to win me to his cause. But thankfully,' he added, a wry smile playing about his lips, 'there are not too many like that.'

That night, in a Havana church, we held our first question-and-answer session. After I had asked a few simple questions about life in Cuba and answered some on the present situation in Holland, I asked if anyone would like to ask me a different type of question.

One man stood up and said, 'Brother Andrew, what must I do to be saved?' I felt a visible change in the atmosphere of the church as I was then able to tell this particular enquirer – with the whole congregation listening as well – how he could be saved by asking God to forgive his sins and then by asking Jesus Christ into his life.

That night, after this unusual service, I invited a group of Cuban pastors to join me for dinner.

As we sat at the table, one leaned over to me and said urgently, 'Brother Andrew, did you bring the plastic bags?'

I smiled.

'Yes, brother, here they are,' I responded as I pulled some from my pockets.

He quickly passed them around the table and as soon as the food was served, the believers began stuffing food into them.

'We couldn't just enjoy this meal by ourselves,' a pastor sitting next to me explained, 'but we also have to share it with our families.

'So we will only eat some of it and take home what is in these bags.'

When the hovering waiters were not looking, I then brought out of my pocket some gifts for them. They were gold goods that I had purchased in Holland. I handed out – under the table – gold wrist and pocket watches.

I had heard that one Christian family in Cuba could live for one month on the value of a wedding ring. So I had bought about £1,000 (US$2,000) worth of jewelry for the trip. I had even left my own wedding ring behind and I had worn one of these gift rings in its place.

'Please, my friends, accept these gifts from the believers of Holland. I want you to sell them and then use the money to support your work and your families.'

Then I looked at José, one of the pastors who I knew had been tortured by the Cuban secret police for his courageous witnessing.

'My brother,' I told him, taking off the gold wedding ring on the third finger of my right hand – the custom in Holland – 'I want you to have this to sell.'

Tears began to trickle from his eyes.

'But, Brother Andrew,' he protested, 'this is your wedding ring, something that is most precious to you.'

I put my arm round his shoulder.

'Brother, this is not my real wedding ring, but a ring I have brought just for you. It symbolises the bond that there is between the believers inside and outside the Sugarcane Curtain.'

His hand was shaking as he took the ring and slipped it on to the third finger on his left hand.

'Thank you, Brother Andrew, for not forgetting us!' His

voice quivered with emotion. 'Tell the people in the West that we also have not forgotten them. We pray for them every day . . . that materialism will not water down their faith.'

Then he smiled. 'This ring will indeed symbolise that we, in the Body of Christ, are all bound together as one – in Jesus Christ.'

12: Pop rivets
and telegram prayers

LONELINESS had become a real problem for me. It was my 'thorn in the flesh'. Travelling for weeks at a time throughout Eastern Europe in my station wagon without company was very difficult. I often felt very isolated.

But by 1965 I thought I had got used to this problem so when I arrived in the United States for my first visit I was knocked sideways by what happened.

For many years I had fought against going there because I felt that was the route many had cynically taken from Europe to pick up finances for their work.

However, I was persuaded to go by an American who was in the audience of a meeting in Holland when I related some of my experiences behind the Iron Curtain.

'Brother Andrew, I think you should come to the United States,' he said, gripping my shoulder. 'The people there should know what is going on in Eastern Europe.'

I suppose I should have realised that something was up when I arrived at this man's theological seminary and saw many of the students carrying rifles.

When I asked one of them why he was armed, he looked at me as if I was mad.

'Don't you realise that the Communists are already at the Mexican border and are planning to invade our country?' he said as he lovingly fingered his weapon of death. 'Brother Andrew, we are proud to fight to the last man.'

In my first meeting there I talked only about the needs of the suffering Church. My backer stormed up to me after I had concluded and shouted, 'Why didn't you slam the Commies?'

'But,' I protested, 'that's not my ministry. I just want to tell the people what is happening to their brothers and sisters behind the Iron Curtain, not attack the system they live under.'

His face was by now blood-red and he shook with anger.

'Well, Brother Andrew, you are no use to me over here. I am cancelling the rest of this trip and you can make your own way back to Holland.'

I was so short of money that I had to stay in the cheapest, most run-down motel I could find. Each morning I would go to a nearby shop, and buy a quart of milk and a yoghurt, which I ate with a shoe horn.

Desperately I contacted Corry in Holland and she wired me some money to stay on a little longer.

Things began to improve – I thought – when I was invited to speak at a large American theological seminary. I used up the last of the money that Corry had sent to pay the air fare to get there. Only three people turned up – a professor and two students. No one even paid my expenses.

After receiving some more financial help from Corry, I managed to pay my fare to speak at a large church in a major American city. As I spoke about the 'Suffering Church' people openly wept in the congregation.

When I had finished, the pastor entered the pulpit and began an impassioned appeal for people to donate money for: new cushion covers for the church. I couldn't believe it. How could he be so unfeeling? It seemed to me that people in the United States were completely selfish. They did not appear interested in the big world outside their borders.

I had never felt so cut off in all my life. Most of the people I met seemed to be completely self-centred. What was God trying to teach me?

One night in Los Angeles, I went along to a meeting to hear a man called John Sherrill speak about his miraculous healing from cancer. Afterwards I was introduced to him and discovered that he had worked for *Reader's Digest* and was now with *Guideposts* magazine in New York.

'Look, Andrew, would you have breakfast with me tomorrow at my hotel?' he asked. 'I'd like to know something of what you have been doing.'

I had never before been in a Hilton Hotel so it was with great nervousness that I entered the lobby of this wondrous place. Our breakfast meeting was really elevating for me. We talked for three hours and John drank in my every word. This was one of the first genuine interests in the 'Suffering Church' I had found from an individual in the United States.

John eventually wrote up the interview for *Guideposts* and the response it generated was phenomenal. And that caused John, along with his wife Elizabeth, to work on my book *God's Smuggler* which has since sold an estimated nine million copies and is now translated into thirty languages and is even distributed secretly in the Soviet Union, China and Cuba.

So the Lord used that time of terrible loneliness in the United States for good – and eventually to considerably further his work to the persecuted Church. With the great interest in the book, more and more people came to join me in my work. Thus the mission *Open Doors with Brother Andrew* was born. I had read in Revelation 3, verse 8, 'Behold, I have set before you an open door, which no one is able to shut . . .' It seemed to me that there should be no closed door to the Gospel, only open ones. So the mission's name stemmed from that conviction I had.

Soon I had many travelling companions. One was Rolph, a dedicated Dutchman. It was during one trip to Moscow with him that I learned the value of telegram prayers. I began to use them on all my border crossings.

One occasion when I really needed a telegram prayer was when I was in the centre of the Russian capital with Rolph. We were in a big delivery van in which I had made panels in the rear and all along the sides to cover up our cargo of 800 Bibles. The only way I could get at those Bibles in Moscow was to drill the hundreds of pop rivets out and then remove the panels.

I told Rolph to keep driving around the Russian capital as I worked feverishly at my task. We had Dutch plates on the car and could have been stopped at any moment by the police especially as Rolph was careering along the roads and through the red lights.

'Not so fast,' I shouted to him, perspiration standing out on my lip. But he just kept going, his foot down on the accelerator, lurching from Red Square to the suburbs and back again. All the time, I kept drilling out those pop rivets.

Suddenly, Rolph screeched to a halt and from my vantage point behind the wafer-thin curtain, I heard a voice bark in Russian, probably saying something like, 'You have just committed a traffic violation.'

I realised immediately that it was a militia man. This was very serious. In an instant I shot up a telegram prayer. 'Lord,' I whispered, 'please blind his eyes.'

I knew that humanly speaking we were well and truly caught like a fly in a spider's web. I had already taken some of the panels off and was filling an old rubber canoe with our contraband Scriptures.

Rolph kept chattering away to the officer in Dutch which obviously confused the man, while I sat in the back hardly daring to breathe.

After a little lecture – most of which we were unable to understand – the policeman hissed an order which I assumed was, 'Get going . . .' Rolph smiled at the man, started up the engine and we were off again on our lurching journey around Moscow, this time at a slightly slower pace. Soon I had all the Bibles out and began popping the new rivets back in and painting over them. It wasn't long before our hair-raising journey was over and the Bibles were transferred from the back of the van into the hands of grateful believers from Moscow's unregistered and therefore illegal Church.

As we handed over the Bibles at a prearranged spot, I said, 'Thank you Lord. You answered my telegram prayer.'

* * *

When our five children were small Corry was not able to join me on trips very often. When they were teengers however she joined me on a visit I was making to Saudi Arabia and the Yemen Arab Republic. I had gone into Saudi to speak to ex-patriots at house meetings and then into the Yemen to meet with missionaries in the capital city of Sana. They were meeting at a special convention there.

Having never travelled in that region before, I was not too prepared for what happened. I managed to persuade the owner of a Land Rover in a town south of Jeddah to take us into the Yemen. At first he didn't seem to think this was a good idea, but the price I promised to pay him when we safely arrived made him change his mind.

Soon we were bumping along through mile after mile of burning desert, occasionally coming to dry river beds. There didn't appear to be any official border between the two countries.

After several hours, I heard the driver let out a yell of terror. I turned and looked ahead and saw a group of men all carrying machine guns.

'Corry, let's begin praying,' I said, my voice high and cracking. 'This could be very dangerous.'

It seemed that these were a group of bandits who required payment before they would let us travel through their 'territory'.

One of them pointed his machine gun at my head and signalled to the others to grab Corry. As they went to take her, one of them pointed to my hands indicating that if there was any trouble from me, they would tie them up behind my back.

'They want to sleep with your wife and then take her to the harem,' spluttered the driver running his long fingers through his lank black hair. 'Then they plan to slit your throat.'

As Corry quietly moved to them she began calmly to say repeatedly to the men, 'God loves you. Jesus loves you. God bless you.' They looked bemused as she went to each of them and said this over and over again.

Telegram prayers were shooting heavenwards from me the whole time Corry was walking among this group of killers.

Suddenly they all broke into wide smiles and their leader signalled to us that we were free to leave.

As we bumped away from this encampment and out into the desert again, I waved to the bandits and then squeezed Corry's hand.

'I was so proud of you,' I told her. 'You were very brave.'

She turned and looked at me. 'Andrew, I wasn't brave at all. The Lord gave me the words to say to those men.'

Her eyes twinkled. 'I have to ask you something, Andrew.'

'Yes, anything.'

'Were you offering up one of your telegram prayers while I was speaking to the men?'

I smiled.

'You know I was . . .'

13: Crash landing

I GASPED in shock as the little plane plummeted downwards at a startling rate. Don, the pilot had taken off all right but then, as we were climbing in the thin air of those Colorado mountains, we started to lose height at great speed.

'What's going on?' I urgently asked Don.

'We're crashing,' was all he could shout before we hit the ground with a jarring thud.

All I can remember was a terrific pain shooting up my back and Don, who had suffered a gaping head wound, saying urgently, 'Andrew, get out and run. The plane could explode at any moment.'

I somehow dragged myself out of the wrecked plane, and tried to run but then collapsed after just a few yards. I didn't know it then, but I had broken my back in two places. As I lay in agony I knew that whether the plane blew up or not, I could not go any further. It was then that I spotted that we had crashed at a spot within yards of a ravine.

As pain enveloped my whole body, I was able to whisper, 'Thank you Lord for sparing our lives.'

In a state of semi-consciousness I saw flashing lights and heard the incessant sound of a siren. I was gently lifted on to a stretcher, and a white-clad medic soothed my brow.

'You'll be okay now, sir. We're taking you to hospital.'

'What about Don?'

'He will be fine. He's going to the same place as you.'

Among the rescuers was a pastor, and he felt that prayer was going to be very important at this time. So he began to phone contacts across the United States asking them to pray for us both. Two well known American Christians who were contacted wee Kathryn Kuhlman and Jamie Buckingham. They immediately passed on the information to delegates at a conference they were all at. Apparently proceedings were stopped so everyone could be in prayer for us.

I was allowed to phone from my hospital bed to Corry in Holland. Within a few days she had flown in and was with me.

'You know, Corry,' I said as she sat at my bedside clasping my hand and fighting back the tears, 'I wonder if the Lord didn't plan all this so I could get right back into the Book.'

'What do youmean, Andrew?' she asked, puzzled.

'Well, I have been so busy delivering Bibles over these years that I have almost forgotten that I, too, need time reading it and letting it soak right into me.

'I've heard that in some parts of Russia a farmer will exchange a cow for one copy of the Scriptures. That's how valuable it is. I wonder if the Lord is telling me how much I need to value his Word?'

Corry nodded her head. 'I know what you mean, Andrew. We get so busy that we don't make time as we should to get into the Scriptures. So why don't we start right now?'

As I lay there in great pain, Corry read aloud chapter after chapter for many hours a day.

God's Word was all I wanted to hear. What a comfort it was to me at that time.

'The Lord is my shepherd . . . I will never leave you nor forsake you . . . be of good cheer for I have overcome the world . . .'

Tears streamed down my cheeks as Corry 'fed' me with God's Word and I heard again those familiar verses of encouragement.

One day as Corry eased me out of bed and took my arm to

help me gingerly walk down the ward, I turned to her and said, 'Darling, don't let me ever forget the story of those American prisoners of war in Vietnam.'

'What story is that, Andrew?'

As we struggled along, I told her of how a number of American soldiers were captured and taken to the north's capital, Hanoi. After they had been kept under strict surveillance for a few weeks, they decided to read to one another from God's Word. They asked one of the guards for a Bible, but the man just shook his head.

'They then decided to write a Bible from memory,' I explained. 'Each soldier quoted the verses he knew from the Bible.

'It started off well. One after another they quoted Bible verses, as one P.O.W. acted as secretary, writing all the verses on a piece of paper.

'Soon, however, they realised how limited their Bible knowledge was. Except for John 3.16, Psalm 23, the "Our Father" and the Ten Commandments, they could only remember a few more verses. They stared at one another. They kept on trying, only to discover that they were confusing one verse with another.'

When we finally got back to my bed, I asked Corry, 'What does that story indicate to you?'

She flicked her Bible open at Colossians 3.16 and read to me, 'Let the word of Christ dwell in you richly . . .'

'That's it, isn't it?' she said. 'Those P.O.W.'s hadn't allowed the Word of God to dwell in them when they had freedom.

'Let that be a lesson to us, Andrew,' Corry continued. 'Never let us be too busy to spend time each day in the Bible. It's vital for our spiritual walk.'

I picked up a leaflet I had been reading. In it I had seen a quote by Dawson Trotman, the founder of the Navigators.

'Corry, let me read what he said. "Nothing yields as much fruit as time devoted to writing God's Word on the tablets of your heart." So let's keep writing . . .'

As I lay in that hospital ward, I learned many new lessons from the Lord. I realised, as I suffered, that I could really identify with Christians who were suffering for their faith. I knew what pain was all about.

One day, Corry read from the Authorised Version, verse 3, chapter 13, of Hebrews.

'Here Andrew, it says, "Remember them that are in bonds, as bound with them; and them which suffer adversity, as being yourselves also in the body."'

I took the Bible from Corry and said, 'It's only when we are really prepared to suffer along with those in the Suffering Church that our prayers on their behalf can reach God's heart.'

'That's right, Andrew. And if you look at verses 18 and 19 you will see that intercessory prayer can get people out of prison.

'You know, I'm sure that the length of the sentence they get is not determined by the judge – though he may think it is – but by praying Christians.'

This was exciting to hear.

'You know, Corry, in future when I pray for a particular prisoner I am going actually to visualise that person in the cell and pray for him as if he were my own son or father.

'I know that God will answer that kind of prayer.'

When I finally returned to Holland I began to put this new kind of prayer into action.

And the more our teams travelled into Eastern Europe, the more I realised how important it was to have believers praying for them.

On a particular occasion, one of our teams was caught with a load of Scriptures by Bulgarian border guards. The team, which comprised a pastor and a doctor, were quizzed for many hours by the police and then put into custody. The clergyman was taken off to prison, but the doctor – a diabetic – was put under house arrest in a hotel room and a guard was posted outside.

The Bulgarian police made one mistake, however. They neglected to disconnect the phone in his room, and so, at three in the morning, he called me.

'Brother Andrew,' he whispered down the receiver, hoping his guard outside was now asleep, 'we've been caught by the Bulgarians and they have locked the pastor up and taken all our Bibles.'

His voice sounded strained and anxious.

'We could be sent to prison for six years if we are found guilty. Please pray and get the whole "family" praying . . . please.'

With that the line went dead. I got out my contacts book and immediately phoned key people in our Open Doors prayer groups around the world. Soon hundreds were on their knees pleading with the Lord to free our brothers in Bulgaria.

I then felt the urge from the Lord to contact my good friend Corrie ten Boom. She had people she knew in a friendly embassy, and despite the fact that it was three in the morning, they began delicate negotiations with the Bulgarians for the release of our men.

With the phoning over, Corry and I got dressed and I drove our car over to visit the nearby families of the pastor and doctor. On both occasions we sat and held hands with them and prayed that the Lord would solve this terrible problem. It wasn't long before I had a wonderful peace about the way this matter was going to be resolved.

'Do you know why I'm no longer worried, Corry?' I asked

as we returned home. 'It's because so many people are interceding.'

Their believing prayers were answered! Three days later the pair were safely back in Holland. As I hugged them they explained that there had been a trial and they were fined and told that they were to lose their car and the load of Bibles, but otherwise they could go free.

'Andrew, it was a miracle,' said the pastor. 'There must have been an awful lot of prayer going up for us at that time . . .'

I nodded and smiled.

'There was . . .'

As well as this new ministry of intercessory prayer, I felt it was also right to be involved in a ministry of encouragement to believers in prison.

I realised how important this was after I had heard that a group of Christians had sent a small box of chocolates to the prison in Leningrad where Aida Skripnikova was sentenced to three years' imprisonment for handing out Gospel literature.

The prison authorities told her about the gift when it arrived, but would not let her have it. After her release Aida said that hearing about the chocolates we sent was as good as getting them simply because she knew others cared.

I told Corry after hearing this, 'I know God will answer the prayer we pray, and also transmit our strength to our suffering brothers and sisters. But first we must be willing to suffer with them.

'You know, that plane crash wasn't pleasant. But I can see God's purpose in it all. I can honestly now say that because of it I have signed up as a fully paid-up member of God's "Suffering Church".'

14: On Idi Amin's 'death list'

IDI Amin was known as the Black Hitler of Africa. He claimed to be a Muslim yet, despite his religious fervour, was one of the most notorious mass murderers in Africa's history.

During his eight-year reign of terror, 'Big Daddy' as he liked to be called, is said to have been responsible for the deaths of 500,000 Ugandans, many of them Christians.

The most publicised of his brutal murders was that of the Anglican Archbishop, Janani Luwum, whom Amin, in a fit of uncontrollable rage, had shot through the mouth.

When I heard of the death of this great Christian, I remembered how I had met him just a short time before his murder.

I had gone to Kampala to meet with Archbishop Luwum to discuss how my organisation, Open Doors, could assist him. As we talked in his home on Namirembe Hill – the name means Hill of Peace – he explained to me that besides being the head of the Church of Uganda, he was also Head Chaplain of the Uganda military forces.

'Brother Andrew, we have a real problem,' he confided. 'We are very short of Bibles for the men. We have many chaplains who are witnessing to the soldiers but have almost no Scriptures to put in their hands.'

I thought for a moment.

'How many do you need?'

The Archbishop didn't have to think for long – he already

knew the answer.

'If you could get us 50,000 Bibles, we could place one in the hands of just about all the servicemen in Uganda.'

I promised him I would do it. So I laid out the need before our supporters in the United States, and within a short time, we had enough contributions to buy and ship some 50,000 Bibles to Uganda.

Now this great leader had been brutally slain by the head of the country that Winston Churchill had once called 'The Pearl of Africa'. The pearl had become tarnished with the blood of thousands of innocent people as Amin's henchmen had run amok in their crusade to set up an Islamic state in a mainly Christian land.

When I heard of Janani's death, I knew I had to go back to Uganda. The Church of Uganda was holding its centenary celebrations and I wanted to be there to show my solidarity with both Janani and the courageous believers there.

The main centenary celebration was to be held in Namirembe Cathedral on June 30, 1977 – one hundred years to the day since the first Anglican missionaries had arrived in Uganda.

This was the second large gathering in the cathedral since Janani's death. The previous one had been an unofficial memorial service to him. The government-controlled radio had announced that a memorial service at the cathedral was forbidden. But still thousands of worshippers went to the ordinary ten a.m. service.

As many people went forward for communion, a soldier rushed up the aisle and pointed out that the clergy were disobeying the directive. He said angrily, 'This service is not supposed to go on.' But the vicar disagreed. 'This is an ordinary service that has been going on for a long time,' he countered.

Someone in the congregation began spontaneously to sing

the Martyrs' Hymn. Everyone joined in and sang it again and again. Then the congregation began slowly moving outside the cathedral and just went on singing. It took an hour for them to file from the cathedral, so great were the numbers. Outside was the empty grave which had been prepared for the Archbishop. However, his body was being flown to his home village of Mucwini, near the Sudan border, for burial.

The people gathered around the open grave site, and retired Archbishop Erica Sabati spoke to the grieving Christians. 'When we see an empty grave, it reminds us of the time when the angels spoke to the women at the empty grave of Jesus on that first Easter, "He is not here. He is risen!"' Sabiti went on to speak of Janani: 'He is not here, but we know that his spirit has gone to be with the Lord Jesus. He is risen! Praise God.'

And while these brave people were risking their lives in memory of their beloved Archbishop, the government-controlled newspaper, *Voice of Uganda*, published a call for President Amin to be made emperor and then proclaimed Son of God.

Now I was in that great cathedral, with my colleagues John and Jan from Holland, for the centenary service. We were the only white people in sight. The atmosphere was so tense that you could reach out and touch the electricity in the air.

I felt goose pimples on my arms as this great body of Christians began to worship the Lord in that beautiful red-brick sanctuary. Archbishop Silvanus Wani, a courageous man who had been elected successor to Janani Luwum, spoke of the 'martyr who died for the nation'. There was utter silence in the church and on the hill outside, which was swarming with people listening to the service on the loudspeaker system.

After the service I tried to arrange a private audience with Idi Amin, but it was called off at the last moment. When I enquired why, I was told by an aide, 'The President for Life cannot see you. He is receiving a new award – Conqueror of the British Empire.'

Nighttime in Kampala was then a dangerous time for everyone. We locked ourselves in our rooms and I went to sleep. But John and Jan found they couldn't.

'What was the problem?' I asked them next morning over breakfast.

'Didn't you hear the screaming?' said an ashen-faced John. 'The State Research men were dragging people from their rooms and taking them away. It was awful.'

While in Kampala I discovered that the Ugandan Christians gave me much more than I was ever able to give them. There were hundreds of thousands of fearless Christians who were totally surrendered to the Holy Spirit. They had a boldness that nothing could quench.

A woman believer came to see us at the Kampala International Hotel which, at that time, was crawling with Amin's so-called secret police. These menacing men from the State Research Bureau were easily identified because most of them wore flowered shirts, dark glasses, bell-bottom trousers and platform-heel shoes.

As the four of us stepped into the lift, I noticed that we were joined by one of these 'secret' policemen, who was taking a great interest in us. He obviously wanted to know what a Ugandan woman was doing with three foreigners. I felt my heart begin to flutter as he stared coldly at us, for I knew that there was more than a possibility that one or all of us could be hauled off to prison.

Suddenly the woman believer smiled broadly at the policeman. Then she opened her handbag, took out a tract and handed it to him.

'Brother, please take this. Jesus loves you and wants to save you,' she said softly. He was greatly taken aback, and as her smile blossomed into an all-consuming grin, he took it. With a flustered look, the policeman stuffed it into his pocket and looked away. That believer had a boldness that could only have come from the Holy Spirit.

My two colleagues and I quickly realised that we were in great danger in Uganda. This was soon confirmed when a Christian leader told us, 'I think you ought to leave as soon as possible. You are all on Amin's death list. It's terribly dangerous for you to stay on any longer.'

We had tickets to leave the next day so we went to the Uganda Airlines terminal in downtown Kampala to re-confirm our flights.

'I'm afraid your names are not on our passenger list,' explained a harassed woman clerk at the desk.

'But our tickets are supposed to be okay,' said Jan. 'Look, we booked them in Kenya. Maybe you could verify this with your computer.'

The clerk smiled in embarrassment.

'Sir, there are *no* computers working in Uganda.'

She then informed us that our names were right at the bottom of the waiting list, with sixteen others above ours.

'But our visas run out tomorrow,' I tried to protest to the clerk.

'Well, that means you will be in trouble then, sir . . .'

We went back to the hotel room and knelt before the Lord. We knew that we were now in a spiritual battle. Idi Amin did not want to let us go. Our thoughts went to our Open Doors prayers partners, who had been alerted around the world to 'intercede' for us on this dangerous mission.

'Lord, lay it upon their hearts to pray for us now,' we pleaded.

We also claimed his promise that he would bountifully

supply all our needs. After all, were we not his ambassadors? Then we should be treated like ambassadors. The plane was to leave at five that afternoon, so we decided to go out to Entebbe Airport as early as possible to see if anything else could be done.

Two other passengers had also arrived early and were standing at the counter where the luggage was to be weighed. Half an hour later, more passengers came and stood behind us. Soon the queue became longer and longer.

The lady who was supposed to give us our seat allocations had still not turned up. It was five o'clock and she wasn't there. Fortunately, we could see the plane, ready for its departure.

Another thirty minutes . . . she finally arrived with a Ugandan soldier at her side. Standing behind the counter, he called out for silence. Immediately all conversation stopped.

'Ladies and gentlemen, please listen carefully. I don't want you to panic. There is a problem. We do not know where the passenger list is. We will start at the front. Those who came first will be helped first.'

Jan and John and myself, were the first to enter the plane. We asked the stewardess where we could sit.

'Take any seat, gentlemen,' she said. 'The plane is yours.' That was true ambassador treatment! 'Thank you, Lord – uh – miss,' said Jan as he sank into the first seat on the aircraft.

Later on I heard how the Lord had laid it on the hearts of our prayer partners to pray for us. 'I thought so much about you and knew you were in trouble,' one sister told me.

That is the reality of a spiritual battle. Our prayer partners were not with us in Uganda, but they knew of our need. They prayed and the passenger list disappeared.

Shortly after Idi Amin had been finally kicked out of Uganda by the Tanzanian Army, Jan went back to Uganda.

One of the first places he visited was the State Research Bureau headquarters at Nakasero where thousands had been brutally killed.

As he was picking his way through the blood-soaked building, he came upon what had once been a secret room. Accompanied by two Tanzanian soldiers, Jan discovered some files strewn across the floor. As he flipped through the pages, he felt all the colour drain from his face. For in there he saw the names of the three of us.

He told me later, 'Brother Andrew, we were indeed on Amin's death list. It was a miracle that we got out on that day.'

15: 'Seek and save' mission to China

A REGULAR travelling companion of mine for several years was Corrie ten Boom, that wonderful Dutch lady who was interned in a German concentration camp during the Second World War for helping to hide Jews. She has told her moving story in the best-selling book, *The Hiding Place*.

During one trip together we were flying into Saigon, South Vietnam, from Bangkok, Thailand. The country was then involved in its terrible war and, as I looked down at the bomb-scarred terrain of that tragic land, Corrie was deeply engrossed in a newspaper.

'Say, Andrew, take a look at this,' Corrie suddenly said, pointing to an article. 'It talks about American soldiers going on what they called "search and destroy" missions.'

She looked at me. 'Search and destroy; that's just the opposite of what Jesus said.' Then she cited Jesus's description of the reason for his coming. '"I am come to seek and to save that which is lost."'

I turned to Corrie and commented, 'I really believe that in this war-like situation in which "search and destroy" has become a watchword, our job as Christians is to "seek and save", and do what Jesus did.'

As we travelled through parts of South East Asia, a new name kept popping up. Different missionaries and Christian leaders who were interested in China told me that an

American ex-Marine called Brother David had been travelling in the opposite direction trying to find depositories where he could leave Bibles at the Chinese borders. Burma was one of his, and my, ports-of-call.

Unfortunately we never met, and so, when I got back to Holland, I penned a letter to Brother David who was then working with the Far East Broadcasting Company in Manila, Phillippines.

It read:

'Dear Brother David,

'Whilst passing through Saigon and Bangkok recently, I heard your name in connection with your recent trip to Burma. As you can imagine, I was deeply interested and very much wanted to see you . . .'

My final paragraph read:

'Please continue the good work, and let us pray that we can meet soon and discuss the work of getting Scriptures into the People's Republic of China.'

Brother David was apparently delighted to get my note and, a few months later, came and stayed with Corry and me in Holland. This former American grid iron footballer with a faith every bit as large as his hulking frame, shared with me his vision for getting Scriptures into the hands of the Chinese.

Brother David told me of the way he had visited countries on the border of China, and found people willing to store Bibles.

'That's great,' I told David, 'but that's not enough. You need to go yourself.'

He looked incredulous, as if I didn't realise that, at that time, America was loathed by the Chinese as the 'Paper Tiger.'

'Brother Andrew,' he said, 'the land is locked tighter than a drum by Mao.'

I smiled.

'It may seem impossible, Brother David, but I want to tell you something that happened to me in 1965.' he looked intently at me as I spoke.

'I had American and Taiwanese visas in my passport and I still got in. If God wants you in, he'll open the door for you to go through.

'And Brother David,' I added, my eyes twinkling, 'I believe the door is already open.''

I shared with him my longing to make contact with the remnant of the Chinese Church, to find out whether it had survived, how it had survived, and what could be done to help and encourage it.

'While I was in Shanghai on my trip, I actually found a Bible bookshop that was still trying to sell Bibles, but could hardly find anyone interested,' I told him sadly.

'The government allowed this funny little place to sell what it considered antiques because it represented no danger. No one cared.

'I tried to hand out Bibles to people but no one would take them. I offered the first one to my interpreter in Canton. She handed it back. She had no time for reading, she said.

'I next tried leaving several "accidentally" behind me in hotel rooms as I checked out. I never succeeded. Always, before I left the floor, the chambermaid would run after me, Bible in hand, and return it to me.

'In desperation, I tried giving Bibles away on the street. My guides made no objection. They seemed in fact to feel sorry for me when person after person stopped to see what I was offering, then gave me the book back.'

The one church I had been able to locate in Peking discouraged me almost as much as the indifference on the streets. In the barren little building I had just seen a tiny group gathered for worship, most of them very old Chinese.

And at the point where their equally elderly pastor delivered his message, all had nodded off to sleep.

'If this was representative of Chinese Christianity, David, I realised their government could stamp it out overnight if they wanted to.'

So was the Church in China dead?

'Certainly, to the outside world, it seems that public religious activity – Christian, Muslim, or Buddhist – has disappeared in China since the Cultural Revolution,' I continued.

'Churches, mosques, monasteries, temples have everywhere been looted and then closed. Many of those places have been turned into factories, warehouses, cinemas and meeting halls. Others have simply been locked and left derelict.

'David, I believe the Lord would have you go and seek out the Church in China. In fact, you need to go on what I like to term a "seek and save" mission.'

I looked at him very seriously. 'Brother David, I believe you should find the Church in China. Locate it. Help it. Encourage it. Feed it. Love it.'

During our time together, we spent hours talking, praying and sharing the Scriptures. Towards the end, he showed me Mark 13.10, where he had been challenged to *publish* abroad the Gospel.

'David,' I asked him, 'what are you really thinking about in terms of Bibles?'

He paused and then launched into his burden.

'I'm praying with my friends in Manila for ten million Scriptures for China.'

He had said it and I could tell that Brother David wanted to see whether or not I would laugh at such an idea.

'Well, from our perspective that may sound like a lot of Bibles,' I began. 'But I am sure in God's eyes it's not so many. Anyway – it's only a small percentage of the present Chinese population.'

Filled with enthusiasm, I said, 'If we can't trust the Lord for such a *tiny* proportion we can't trust him for anything. I stand with you in that vision, Brother David.'

* * *

The crew of the tug-boat Michael sent in a cryptic message to a group of Chinese believers in Swatow: 'We are going to have a dinner party, expecting so many people that we have arranged twenty-one teacups and cooked eighteen bowls of rice.'

It was June 18, 1981, Project Pearl was underway. One million Bibles were going to be taken in to China as part of our vision to see ten million Scriptures eventually go in. Since I had first spoken to him Brother David had made many trips inside the People's Republic of China and he and his dedicated team of workers had uncovered a vibrant Church in China that had survived unparalleled persecution. Our contacts inside gave us information that leads us to believe there could be twenty million believers in hundreds of thousands of house churches across the country.

Now they were poised to make what must have been the biggest Bible delivery of its kind in history. When the team from many countries around the world arrived at that strip of moonlit beach they planned to unload the 323 ton cargo of one million Bibles and float them to land with the help of fast rubber boats.

Once the mission was over Brother David was able to give me a detailed report of what happened. He told me that as they approached the beach, a Chinese patrol boat with a manned machine gun on its stern deck headed straight for the tugboat that was towing the barge Gabriella that contained the huge cargo of Bibles.

'I told the Lord that there was nothing we could do,' Brother David said. 'Only he could take control of the situation. I knew that he loved those believers waiting for us on that beach and he wanted his Word to be put in their hands.'

The boat miraculously went straight by – as if God had blinded the eyes of its Chinese crew.

As the Open Doors group arrived at Swatow Beach, 200 miles up the Chinese coast from Hong Kong, the captain, Karl, cut the engines. It was the beginning of a night to be remembered. The crew knew that around the world thousands of believers had been alerted and were praying for them.

However, they hadn't realised the size of their welcome on the beach. Some several thousand Chinese believers were there to meet them and receive the valuable cargo of Union version Bibles printed in China's new simplified script – the version which had been particularly requested by believers.

So David, along with Joseph Lee, his Chinese co-worker, and American colleague, Pastor Ward, climbed over the side of the tug.

'Waiting for us in the rubber "Z" boat below were Pablo, a Canadian, and Australian Michael Bruce, two more Open Doors co-workers.

'Our little boat surged towards the shore and as we approached I recalled the way that one old lady, Grandmother Kwang, had prayed on the beach every night for this moment.

'The "Z" boat reached the shallows, and we jumped into the water. Wading towards us with arms outstretched were the leaders of the Chinese believers. Dispensing with traditional Chinese reserve, they leapt into our arms, hugging each of us in turn.

'Then, with the water lapping around our feet, one of

them delivered a carefully rehearsed English greeting.

'"Welcome to China, Uncles,"' he said, his bright eyes reflecting the moonlight. Others delivered the same message in succession.

Despite the joy of the occasion there was a sense of urgency about the task in hand. After a few minutes prayer my walkie-talkie crackled into life and we were underway.'

Brother David explained that after that everything happened at once.

'Our barge had been partially flooded during the preceding hour to lower it according to the plan. Now additional water was pumped into one side to bring it down to water level,' he said.

'Half of the barge was lowered and, with the assistance of the men, the huge one-ton blocks of Bibles were manhandled into the water. Massive ropes were attached from the top of each one-ton package to the bottom of the base of the next and they fell domino-like on to the smooth surface.

'The "Z" boats then sprang into life as the blocks spread out, the rubber crafts guiding them to shore.

'I'll never forget the moment the first blocks reached the beach. Although they knew what to expect, there was still a sense of disbelief as the believers cut them open and held the boxes of Bibles close, their eyes brimming with tears.

'Sheer joy rendered them speechless as Ooooooh's and Aaaaah's echoed over the sand. Finally, they found their tongues and praised God, their voices ringing with absolute delight.

'They fingered the Bibles over and over with faces alight. Well before the delivery these people had told us they would be willing to die to see the Word of God come to their land. Now they held it in their hands.'

Mindful of the danger of discovery, the work went ahead

at great speed. Inside each one-ton block were forty-eight boxes, containing ninety Bibles apiece.

'We had deliberately chosen this size box so that the local Christians would be able to carry them two at a time suspended from a traditional over-shoulder bamboo-pole,' Brother David continued.

Eventually, the Chinese leaders urged Brother David and his crew to leave. Earlier that day the believers had seen soldiers combing the beach after a robbery in the area.

'They wanted to get us away as quickly as possible in case a second patrol was planned for that night,' he said.

'The tug's engine sprang into life as we said goodbye to our Chinese family, after two hours in which I had sensed God's presence more acutely than ever in my life before. Despite the fatigue, every man on board was bursting to sing for joy. We knew we had been with Jesus. And we had seen him at work in such a way that we felt we had been spectators as much as participants.

After Brother David and his crew left, soldiers came to the beach and eyewitnesses later told us that a total of 10,000 Bibles were destroyed – one percent of the delivery.

Brother David has since received detailed reports from Chinese believers that seem to indicate that all the remaining Bibles from the beach delivery are now in the hands of the believers all over the People's Republic of China. Counting also Bibles delivered by other means during the project we had completed our Project Pearl goal of one million Bibles delivered to China.

And what was the response from inside China of that night to be remembered? Brother David showed me a letter from one of the leaders who was on the beach that night.

It read: 'Ink and pen are unable to describe his wonderful works, nor tongues his power. How my heart moves, but pen and paper are unable to express my feelings . . . that night, Jehovah appeared to us by the beach and reigned as King.'

The whole delivery, as far as the Open Doors crew involvement was concerned, took under two hours and by then part of God's Church in China had been 'fed' in a wonderful new way.

It was a 'seek and save' mission that none of us will ever forget! A pearl of great price for the believers of the most populous nation in the world.

---

*The full story of Brother David's ministry to China is told in *God's Smuggler to China*, published by Hodder and Stoughton.

16: God's special agents

SOME time ago I applied to join the Not Terribly Good Club of Great Britain. Why? Quite simply because I believe I *am* a failure.

You have read in this book about my first real flop which took place in 1953 when I arrived in Britain from my native Holland to study at the Worldwide Evangelisation Crusade's Glasgow College. It was when Uncle Hoppy used to make me preach to a row of empty chairs in his mission hall.

So I was a real failure in those days. I couldn't even draw a crowd.

I had another failure soon after I got involved in Bible smuggling into Eastern Europe. I have also recounted the story of when I was 'caught' with my precious cargo at the East German border between West Berlin and East Germany. At Helmstadt, an officer came and I had to admit I had Bibles in my car.

I actually wanted to join the British-based failure club so I could be its chaplain. I wanted to tell the failures of this world about Jesus Christ who apparently failed in his mission because he was killed on the cross.

But did he really fail? I wanted to explain that Jesus actually turned failure into victory by that death.

Sadly, however, the club has now failed. Stephen Pile, the founder of the club, had an unfortunate break which resulted in his being thrown out of his own organisation.

His *Book of Heroic Failures* got into the best-sellers' list in England, making him an overnight success.

This got me thinking how we, as Christians, have largely failed our suffering brothers and sisters around the world. One of my favourite verses in the Bible is found in Revelation, chapter 3, verse 2, 'Awake, and strengthen what remains and is on the point of death . . .'

We need to wake up to the needs of believers who are 'at the point of death'. Do you realise that more people have been killed for their faith in Jesus Christ in the twentieth century than in all the previous centuries put together? At least sixty per cent of the world's population now lives under totalitarian regimes that threaten or have already taken away their freedom.

In the West we are spending billions of pounds in arming ourselves against the threat of Communist countries, but I believe we are wrong in some of our thinking.

Some years ago I had the opportunity to speak at a meeting of the chiefs of staff of the United States Army, Navy and Air Force at the Pentagon in Washington D.C.

I told them, 'I am convinced that if the Pentagon would designate one per cent of the United States Defence Budget to provide Bibles to Russia and China, then you would not need to spend the other ninety-nine per cent on defence.'

I could see some of those there were squirming in their seats and they obviously did not agree with what I had said. After I had spoken several of those 'Top Brass' came over to shake my hand.

One told me, 'Brother Andrew, I think I agree with your statement.'

I looked into his eyes and said, 'Well, why don't you do something about it?'

He gestured to indicate that he couldn't. The decision did not lie with him.

But back to my failures.

You will remember that I left the W.E.C. college without

a diploma. I failed dismally as a student, yet God was still able to use me once I had submitted to his will. I am not urging any of you to abandon your studies, but I feel it is possibly better for you to learn a trade or profession before considering Bible college.

I find so many young people, once they have become Christians, want to become full-time workers. Well, be careful.

I have warned thousands of young people not to *desire* to become 'full-timers' in Christian work. The problem is that many people feel only then are they doing something special in the Kingdom of God.

In reality, there are many unhappy servants of God who would be much happier and more effective if they had stayed in their secular jobs and lived and witnessed for the Lord there.

When I first became a Christian, I was working in a chocolate factory in the Dutch district of Alkmaar. I was enthusiastic, and won people there for Christ.

I remember when I first arrived at the factory, which produced high-quality bon bons, many of which were exported to the United States and Germany, I couldn't believe the behaviour of the girls there. The dirty jokes and swear words were much worse than I had ever heard in the Dutch army in the East Indies.

One particularly shy office worker there was Corry, who was later to become my wife. Corry told me how she used to watch me witness and live out the Christian life in the boring job I had been given.

In spite of the crude atmosphere in that factory, God did a great work there and so many eventually came to know Christ that two years later I had to tell some of those same girls not to read their Bibles during working hours.

I must admit that in the first years of being a full-timer I didn't have nearly as much blessing as I used to have in the factory. Many times I prayed to the Lord, 'Please send me back to that chocolate factory.'

I am not against young people being full-time in the Lord's work but I am against the *desire* of young people to be full-timers. You should only go full-time if there is no other way out. It should be as Paul expressed it: 'The need is laid upon me, I have no choice' (see 1 Corinthians 9:16, 17).

You see, God is preparing our hearts for the highest service. At whatever level you are now, God is preparing you for still higher service. There will never be a time when this preparation will stop.

When my earlier book, *God's Smuggler*, appeared, I admit that I wasn't completely happy with that title. Like many other people, I associated bad things such as narcotics with smuggling. Besides that, it implies the negative idea of breaking the law. But the word has stuck, and so I accept it, though it has certainly caused some wild notions about what we do.

We are not some kind of spiritual stunt men who go careering recklessly around Eastern Europe with our little station wagons full of Bibles trying to see how much we can get away with and not get caught. The plight of our persecuted brethren is far too desperate for us to pull tricks just for the fun of showing off.

What we really are is *special agents* of a government not of this world. We do everything we can to promote the cause of our sovereign Lord, whether we are allowed to do it in the open or are forced to do it under cover.

Perhaps the whole thing is redeemed by being linked with God: if indeed I am a smuggler, it is to do God's work among God's people with God's supplies and according to God's orders. Actually, labels make little difference. What matters is that we obey the Lord.

The thing that got me going all of those years ago was hearing about a Communist youth movement with 96 million members. The number in those young Communist leagues has now swelled to 120 million members, making it by far the largest organisation of its sort in the world. As faithful followers of their party line, these young people are being trained for world revolution and they are going to risk their lives to succeed.

Years ago, when Kruschev was still in power, he stood in Red Square in Moscow and spoke with very scriptural words to the massed troops of the Russian army: 'You are all dead men!' He implied that in principle they had already lost their lives to the party. Then he added: 'Now go into the world and prove it!'

In effect, Christ said that to his disciples.

We will never conquer Communism as long as we put our trust in men. It is a spiritual power and it can be opposed and overcome only by another spiritual power. Which other spiritual power is available? The Church of Christ!

Therefore, in those countries where the Church of the Lord Jesus is being suppressed, persecuted, and almost wiped out (the official church, at least, in Albania, in North Korea, and Tibet – three Communist countries without any church) we have to be especially under divine obligation to step in and do something that their governments strongly disagree with, that is highly illegal from their point of view. We have got to do it for the sake of Christ and for the sake of the whole world for which he died.

That is our position in our mission. That's why I don't want to argue for long with people who say that smuggling is immoral. I don't want to waste my time. We have the great commission and command to go in and preach Christ's deliverance to the captives; to win others to the Lord – yes, to win Communists for Christ! To do all that requires, first of all, that we strengthen the brethren.

It *is* a spiritual battle. Therefore, we must become spiritual people, and must see the spiritual principles involved before we can be of any use, before we can effectively minister in this world.

Are you willing to join in the battle? Are you willing to become one of God's special agents? Do it today!

17: Are you ready for action

THIS is my most important question for you. Have you often prayed, 'Oh God, use me in your service; send people across my path with whom I can share the Gospel?' God longs to answer that prayer, but nothing will happen unless you are prepared to act. It is only the car which is in motion which can be steered in the right direction, even if it does move off in the wrong direction at first. Never be afraid of making mistakes – the greatest mistake is to sit down and wait for guidance and a call which can never reach us. So let us continually present ourselves to God so that he can use us for the great plans he has for the countries we live in. *Act* on the steps I suggest below, for unless you take the initiative, *nothing* will change.

The local church

Begin where you are: offer your services to your local pastor or minister. One of the most important aspects of serving the Lord is your ability to do so in the local church. If you cannot work well at home, you will not work well anywhere else. The local church is a workshop for in-service training, it is not a rest home for the saints! In Acts 13 we find that Paul and Barnabas were called while ministering in the local church. They had become indispensable, and this qualified them for a wider ministry. Only those who are missed with regret will be received with joy. Make sure therefore, that you become indispensable in your local church, not because of all the work done in committees, but through being directly involved in some type of evangelism.

Broaden your interests

In your town there may be some interdenominational work such as Youth for Christ, The Navigators, The Bible Society, Gideons International, Operation Mobilisation, Youth With A Mission, or even a Christian businessmen's group. Experience working with a group like one of these would be excellent preparation for work in other countries. There may be some areas where your local church has no outreach. Find out about these, and try to do something there.

Do something new

Do something you have never done before . . . for example:

Call the children in your street together and arrange an attractive meeting. This automatically leads to contact with parents. Try to do this weekly, with emphasis on evangelism. Your local Sunday School and organisations like Scripture Union and Scripture Press could help you.

Always have a Gospel tract ready to give away, and make sure you have tracts which apply to different situations. The Scripture Gift Mission could supply you with excellent materials. Make sure that you have given a printed witness to all whose who work with you. If we have not told those close to us about Jesus Christ, how shall we ever tell those who live far off?

Start a prayer group – even one other Christian is enough to begin with – in your own home or with your colleagues at work, for example, with nurses and medical personnel in hospitals, with fellow soldiers in the barracks, with students at University, with work-mates at the office or factory. Why not write to your local Open Doors office whose address is at the back of this book? Tell them that you want to start a prayer group for the Suffering Church and our ministry in particular and they will be glad to supply you with a regular prayer cassette.

Study your Bible

When you start doing these things, you will find that you do not know the Bible well enough. In my own experience, it was while I was giving out that I found how little I knew. Often, after making house calls or speaking with people on the streets, I would go back to my study feeling defeated. This forced me to further prayer and Bible study. You will experience this as well. I therefore recommend four things:

Discipline yourself to a life of prayer. If you discipline yourself in the beginning, the end will take care of itself. You can never be God's mouthpiece if you have not learned to listen first.

Study the Bible for yourself. I would advise you to read your Bible through at least once a year. This amounts to only three chapters every weekday and five chapters on Sundays – not as much as most people read when they pick up the daily newspaper!

To get much more out of the Bible, I recommend Bible study books, such as those offered by The Navigators, which work systematically through the books and doctrines of the Bible.

Read as many good Christian books as you can. We especially recommend missionary biographies, and the writings of such outstanding men of God as C. T. Studd, Andrew Murray, Watchman Nee, Hudson Taylor, Oswald Smith and Oswald Chambers.

Learn a profession or trade first

To young people seeking the Lord's will for full-time

service we would give this advice . . . learn a profession or a trade first of all. This is a day of specialisation and more and more doors are being closed to the traditional type of missionary work, but no doors are really closed if we have specialised training – in linguistics, archaeology, diplomacy, or in the medical, agricultural, technical or journalistic fields. Too many young people have stopped their training in secular work in their first missionary enthusiasm, and have gone straight into missionary work, many of them to regret it later, as their secular skills would have been of tremendous assistance in the Lord's work. We must bear in mind the words of our Lord in Mark 12.30 where Jesus tells us that the first commandment is to 'love the Lord your God with all your heart, and with all your soul, and with all your mind, and with all your strength.' Here God places as much emphasis upon 'mind' as he does upon 'strength' and 'heart'.

Missionary training

The next stop is obviously to undertake some definite missionary training. There are many Bible schools and missionary training colleges. Young people with limited time available who desire involvement with worldwide evangelistic movements may contact groups like Operation Mobilisation, Youth with a Mission, Campus Crusade for Christ, The Navigators, and those organisations that are involved in child evangelism.

Many young people who have been involved in this type of short-term ministry have often gone into full-time service afterwards. God has shown us that he can and does use ordinary men and women to do his work, but we must give him the opportunity to show us first. My advice, therefore, is always to 'get involved'.

Four definite requirements

As is the case with all missionary opportunities, there are four definite requirements . . . that you should be:

> physically fit
> emotionally stable
> spiritually mature
> professionally competent

Our mission field calls for dedicated specialists, men and women who will fight, plod, suffer, and in it all, maintain their faith in the all-victorious Son of God who calls them! There is a big job to be done, and we must do it well, 'preaching the Kingdom of God, and teaching those things which concern the Lord Jesus Christ, with all confidence, no man forbidding' (Acts 28.31).

Once again I ask you, are you ready for action? Are you willing to become a special agent for God?

If you want to know more of the ministry of *Open Doors with Brother Andrew* write to the following addresses:

Open Doors with Brother Andrew,
P.O. Box 6,
Standlake,
Witney,
Oxon,
OX8 7SP,
England.

Or:
Open Doors International,
P.O. Box 47,
3840AA Harderwijk,
Holland.

Other books by Brother Andrew
God's Smuggler *(with John and Elizabeth Sherrill)*
The Ethics of Smuggling
Battle for Africa *(with Charles Paul Conn)*
Building in a Broken World

Edited by Brother Andrew
Destined to Suffer?

Other books by Dan Wooding
Junkies Are People Too
Stresspoint
I Thought Terry Dene Was Dead
Exit the Devil *(with Trevor Dearing)*
Train of Terror *(with Mini Loman)*
Rick Wakeman, the Caped Crusader
King Squealer *(with Maurice O'Mahoney)*
Guerrilla for Christ *(with Salu Daka Ndebele)*
Uganda Holocaust *(with Ray Barnett)*
Miracles in Sin City *(with Howard Cooper)*
God's Smuggler to China *(with Brother David and Sara Bruce)*
Prophets of Revolution *(with Peter Asael Gonzalez)*